T0323822

SIMONE DE BEAUVOIR
THE BASICS

Simone de Beauvoir: The Basics provides an accessible introduction to the life, work, and ground-breaking ideas of author, philosopher, and feminist Simone de Beauvoir.

The book offers readers "the basics" of Beauvoir, affording new and continuing readers a guide to her works and ideas. The book examines the main developments in her life, the social and political events and efforts, as well as intellectual figures who influenced her thinking. Readers will be introduced to her existentialist ethics of freedom and her preoccupation with situations of oppression, covering her more widely read philosophical texts like *The Second Sex* and *The Ethics of Ambiguity*, as well as her lesser-known texts like *A Very Easy Death* and *Les Belles Images*.

Simone de Beauvoir: The Basics offers an energetic introduction to Beauvoir that encourages readers to study her further and will inspire them to think with Beauvoir in their own lives, and is of value to those studying Beauvoir's work for the first time and those looking for a supplement to their general knowledge of Beauvoir.

Megan Burke is Associate Professor of Philosophy at Sonoma State University and has published extensively on Beauvoir in venues such as Feminist Theory, Hypatia, and Simone de Beauvoir Studies.

THE BASICS SERIES

The Basics is a highly successful series of accessible guidebooks which provide an overview of the fundamental principles of a subject area in a jargon-free and undaunting format.

Intended for students approaching a subject for the first time, the books both introduce the essentials of a subject and provide an ideal springboard for further study. With over 50 titles spanning subjects from artificial intelligence (AI) to women's studies, *The Basics* are an ideal starting point for students seeking to understand a subject area.

Each text comes with recommendations for further study and gradually introduces the complexities and nuances within a subject.

For a full list of titles in this series, please visit www.routledge.com/The-Basics/book-series/B

SIMONE DE BEAUVOIR

THE BASICS

Megan Burke

LONDON AND NEW YORK

Designed cover image: © Getty Images

First published 2025
by Routledge
4 Park Square, Milton Park, Abingdon, Oxon OX14 4RN

and by Routledge
605 Third Avenue, New York, NY 10158

Routledge is an imprint of the Taylor & Francis Group, an informa business

British Library Cataloguing-in-Publication Data
A catalogue record for this book is available from the British Library

Library of Congress Cataloging-in-Publication Data
Names: Burke, Megan, 1983- author.
Title: Simone de Beauvoir : the basics / Megan Burke.
Description: Abingdon, Oxon ; New York, NY : Routledge, 2024. | Series: The basics | Includes bibliographical references and index.
Identifiers: LCCN 2024007423 (print) | LCCN 2024007424 (ebook) | ISBN 9781032508634 (hardback) | ISBN 9781032508610 (paperback) | ISBN 9781003399995 (ebook)
Subjects: LCSH: Beauvoir, Simone de, 1908–1986—Criticism and interpretation. | LCGFT: Literary criticism.
Classification: LCC PQ2603.E362 Z6216 2024 (print) | LCC PQ2603.E362 (ebook) | DDC 194—dc23/eng/20240422
LC record available at https://lccn.loc.gov/2024007423
LC ebook record available at https://lccn.loc.gov/2024007424

ISBN: 978-1-032-50863-4 (hbk)
ISBN: 978-1-032-50861-0 (pbk)
ISBN: 978-1-003-39999-5 (ebk)

DOI: 10.4324/9781003399995

Typeset in Sabon
by codeMantra

To Bonnie and Debra.

CONTENTS

PREFACE

Although one of the most important intellectuals of the twentieth century, most people do not know much about Simone de Beauvoir. I hope this book changes that. My hope is that this book offers an exciting introduction to Beauvoir for those who are reading her work for the very first time, as well as for those who are continuing to read her work but desire to know more about her ideas and *oeuvre*. Whether you are attending a course in which Beauvoir's work is assigned to you or whether you are inspired to pick up her work for personal enrichment, I hope this book entices you to think with Beauvoir further.

Since the circumstances in which she grew up and lived are formative to her work more generally, the book begins with a consideration of Beauvoir's life and influences. Her proclivity for the genre of life writing suggests that there is philosophical significance in narrating a life. As we will see, her life was both ordinary and epic, relatable and extraordinary, which, in my view, makes her ideas relevant and exciting. Every subsequent chapter is framed by issues and themes that preoccupied Beauvoir throughout her lifetime. In every chapter, you will be introduced to concepts central to her lexicon, which I have bolded to make them stand out, and you will gain a basic understanding of key works. At the end of each chapter, I also offer resources for further reading, allowing you to more thoroughly pursue topics and texts that peak *your* interest. The chapters are written to build on one another, but it is also possible to read each chapter individually or when it is convenient for your studies. While a book cannot be everything to everyone, I have done my best to make this book friendly and useful to a variety of readers with diverse interests and needs.

I know the first time I read Beauvoir in a feminist theory course at the age of 19, I never thought that decades later I would be writing a book about her. But that is a testament to the impact and intrigue of her work. By the end of this book, you may not be willing to call yourself a Beauvoirian, but I hope you'll at least come to agree that Simone de Beauvoir's writings and the ideas she formulated are worthy of our attention.

ACKNOWLEDGMENTS

Certain material conditions and the support and love of others make thinking and writing possible. I was fortunate to write most of this book while on sabbatical from Sonoma State University and with a courtesy research appointment from the University of Oregon. Both conditions afforded me time, space, and personal and intellectual well-being, which are indispensable to conceiving and writing a book. I have been equally fortunate to think alongside and learn from brilliant Beauvoir scholars for over a decade, including but not limited to Sarah LaChance Adams, Meryl Altman, Ellie Anderson, Debra Bergoffen, Bonnie Mann, Qrescent Mali Mason, Jennifer McWeeny, Tove Pettersen, Dana Rognlie, Margaret Simons, and Gail Weiss. I'm grateful for your work and for the ways it has pushed me to know Beauvoir better. To the Beauvoir scholars I have not mentioned, including the ones I do not know personally—I am equally as indebted to your work. Thanks to all of you for making the world of Beauvoir studies a rich, intellectual community. I am grateful to the undergraduate students in my existentialism class at Sonoma State during the spring 2022 semester. Thank you for reading Beauvoir with me, and for your excellent questions about and critiques of her work.

It would be remiss not to mention that I would likely not have ever read Beauvoir, or at least read her in the ways I came to if it had not been for Debra Bergoffen's willingness to do an independent study with me as an undergraduate student. That early interest was later nurtured by Bonnie Mann whose graduate seminar on Beauvoir revealed dimensions to her work that I had not considered. By matter of chance, my doctoral studies of Beauvoir coincided with the publication of the 2010 English translation of *The Second Sex*. Being immersed in the conversations and tensions with longstanding Beauvoir scholars at such a pivotal time in my academic career was impactful. Thank you to all of those who were willing to involve a younger scholar in longstanding debates, and for offering a model of intellectual community guided by passion and complexity. To Dana, thank you for reading Beauvoir with me, always, at any time, even sometimes over text, and supporting my own readings and claims about her ideas, while also challenging me with your own. The intellectual companionship we've created around Beauvoir is a real gift, personally and professionally.

I would not have been able to retreat into the ideas contained in this book, or into myself to think about them, were it not for some special connections in my life. To Angela, Arian, Eric, Gonzalo, Heather, Jeff, Maia, Matt, Rebekah, and Tish—thank you for showing up for me in the unique ways you did as I wrote this book. Your interests in my freedom, in my joy, and in who I am were, and still are, invaluable. For those of you who listened to me go off about Beauvoir's life and works— thank you. For those of you who read chapters to learn more and get to know me better—thank you. For those of you who pushed me to laugh, dance, or do anything else other than think and write about Beauvoir—thank you. In the absence of having such a rich and loving relational world, my early morning writing sessions would not have been as easy and fun. Thanks to each of you for supporting my project and responding to my appeal. To my pups, Lily and Jonsi, thanks for getting me outside and away from books and my computer, and for laying across my lap while I wrote. Most importantly, mom—I'm grateful for you reading every chapter of this book to learn, grow, and understand me in yet another way. You never cease to show me what it is to love in ways that open the future for another.

WHO IS SIMONE DE BEAUVOIR?

Simone de Beauvoir was a prolific author and philosopher, an influential feminist and leftist activist, and one of the major figures in existentialism in post-WWII France. She authored numerous literary works, philosophical essays and books, political essays, as well as newspaper articles, and toured the world as a public intellectual. She lived through major social and political changes, including WWI and WWII, inspired the feminist movement of the mid-twentieth century, and defied social expectations and conventions in how she lived. Simone de Beauvoir lived a bold life, intellectually, politically, and personally, carving out a place for herself in and after her lifetime as one of the twentieth century's most well-known intellectual women.

Yet, during her lifetime and for years after her death, Beauvoir was not held in the high esteem she deserved. She was not regarded as a central figure in French existentialism and phenomenology, two forms of philosophical inquiry. She was overshadowed by her male contemporaries, Albert Camus, Maurice Merleau-Ponty, and especially Jean-Paul Sartre. When her philosophical work was recognized, it was generally in relation to Sartre, her longtime lover and intellectual companion. Her ideas, it was said, were really his. As Beauvoir's analysis of women's existence in *The Second Sex* makes clear, relegating Beauvoir's status and refusing her originality, while admiring the lives and ideas of men is a patriarchal standard. That Beauvoir was a woman who operated in a domain historically reserved for white men and that, in her writing, she

DOI: 10.4324/9781003399995-1

centered women's experiences and perspectives that challenged dominant values and conventions were grounds for rejecting her work or demoting its brilliance.

This is not to say that Beauvoir's work did not receive any recognition during her lifetime. When *The Second Sex* was published in 1949 it was met with public outrage because of the way Beauvoir criticized and challenged the patriarchal status quo. For many women readers, however, they saw in Beauvoir a woman speaking to them, about their experience, in ways that resonated and ignited feminist consciousness. Her popularity and influence among her feminist readers made her a feminist icon of the twentieth century. And, in 1954, upon publication of her novel *The Mandarins*, she was awarded the *Prix Goncourt*, a prestigious prize in French literature. She also toured various countries, often with Sartre but sometimes alone, as a French intellectual, giving lectures and interviews on her views on existentialism, freedom, and oppression. The fact of the matter is that throughout her lifetime Beauvoir formulated new answers to classic philosophical questions, such as: What is freedom? Why do something rather than nothing? How should we live in a world with others? But she also formed her own way of doing philosophy, which allowed her to tend to experiences seen as philosophically insignificant, including the subordination of women and old age.

While the bulk of this book will focus on her ideas, we will begin by taking a closer look at her life and intellectual motivations. Her life is just as much a part of her intellectual contributions as are her actual works. Far from an armchair philosopher, Beauvoir's work is grounded and emergent in the life she lived.

THE LIFE OF SIMONE DE BEAUVOIR

Simone de Beauvoir was born on January 9, 1908, in the sixth arrondissement in Paris, France, the district where Beauvoir would live out most of her life. She was the first child of Françoise Brasseur and Georges Bertrand de Beauvoir who had married on December 21, 1906. Françoise and Georges descended from the same privileged social class. Initially, their class status allowed them to adopt a bourgeois, Parisian life, but at the time of Beauvoir's birth the family wealth was in the process of decline as Françoise's father could not pay her dowry. Years later, after WWI, Georges would squander the family's cash in bad investments. This financial reality meant that the family would live in the economic moderation of the middle class, rather than the luxuries of the upper echelons of the French bourgeoisie. Two and half years after Beauvoir's birth, her sister, Henriette-Hélène de Beauvoir was born. Although they had taken pride in the birth of their first daughter, Françoise and Georges, longing for their second child to be a son, were expressively disappointed. Hélène, nicknamed and most often called Poupette (meaning "little doll"), quickly became second to her older sister. As Beauvoir in the first volume of her autobiography, *Memoirs of a Dutiful Daughter*, writes, "I had never been compared to anyone: she was always being compared with me ...whatever Poupette might do, and however well she might do it, the passing of time and the sublimation of the legend all contributed to the idea that I [Simone] had done everything much better" ([1958] 1959, 45).

In Beauvoir's early years, Françoise and Georges raised their eldest daughter against the grain. Rather than discipline her into the obedience expected from a young girl, Françoise and Georges entertained their smart, stubborn, and capricious daughter, and encouraged her opinionated, independent disposition. This treatment of Beauvoir allowed her to become a self-assured girl. Françoise and Georges also introduced their young daughter to the world of books, cultivating an early intellectual development. Georges took much pride in his daughter's early signs of intelligence and regularly supplied Beauvoir with books and encouraged a passion for reading. The young Beauvoir was also passionate about writing. She kept diaries and wrote stories throughout her girlhood. She wrote, by hand, her first surviving story at age seven, which was one hundred pages long.

This more expansive dimension of Beauvoir's rearing was not absolute. She and her sister were raised to revere Catholic values and ideals. Although their father was not a devout Catholic and therefore did not abide by its morality, her mother, who, like most women, was responsible for much of the girls' upbringing, was committed to Catholic morality. Françoise was, in fact, rigid in her Catholicism, which meant a strict adherence to its moral and social conventions. The Catholic dichotomy of Good and Evil came to have an overbearing presence in their life. They participated in Catholic rituals like Sunday Mass, prayer, and strict etiquette overseen and enforced by their mother. As a result, Beauvoir came to believe she must live a life of devotion, sacrifice herself for others, be dutiful to God, become a devoted mother and wife, and she learned that the body, and a woman's body in particular, was to be concealed. Françoise also vetted Beauvoir's childhood friends, making sure she was in the company of "proper" influence.

Initially, Beauvoir took to her Catholic rearing. She took to the vocation of becoming a well-mannered and devoted Catholic girl. Even while her religious devotion may have been stifling in certain respects, she credits it with helping her question societal views of girls. Her soul was no more valuable to God than a boy's soul and therefore her existence as a girl must certainly not be any less important than a boy's. Her relationship to her faith began to change in adolescence, however. In some respects, this change had to do with her and Poupette's relationship to their mother. The girls found her to be tyrannical and unbearable. In response, the sisters invented a private language and played games in made-up worlds to challenge the overarching presence of their mother and to imagine themselves beyond the constraints of their middle class, Catholic upbringing.

Throughout her childhood, Beauvoir experienced herself and her life at the crossroads of freedom and constraint. She was encouraged to be curious, smart, and independent, but she was also required to accept the will of God without question and lead a life of self-sacrifice. And, as she neared adolescence, her parents judged her in conventional ways. Her father, for instance, judged her for her appearance, even as he had also once proudly asserted, "Simone has a man's brain; she thinks like a man she *is* a man." As she would go on to describe in several of her works, living under the authority of adults and their implacable values afforded her a shelter of safety and the ability to live carefree. But she also had her suspicions. At times she strove to be independent while at others she felt herself to be docile and obedient to the will of others. As philosopher Kate Kirkpatrick, one of Beauvoir's biographers, remarks in *Becoming Beauvoir* (2019), "How to resolve these conflicting desires—to live a life of devotion to others or to live life for oneself—was to become one of the central questions" of Beauvoir's work (45).

Beauvoir lived during a time in which girls and women could pursue opportunities they had previously been denied, including access to education. At the age of five and half, Beauvoir began attending the Institut Adeline Désir (which she called Le Cours Désir), a private Catholic school for girls. Beauvoir's attendance at the school had much to do with the decline in her family's class status, since the children from the upper class received private tutelage at home. This was a fortunate circumstance for Beauvoir. Le Cours Désir was one of the few schools to encourage young women to complete baccalaureate exams, which qualify a student for access to higher education. It was as a student at Le Cours Désir that Beauvoir decided she wanted to become a teacher. Once again, the class decline of her parents had its benefits. Since her father would not have a dowry to provide a potential husband, Beauvoir needed to become economically independent, which a teaching career would provide. Françoise and Georges were on board with their daughter's career aspirations as a result. The opportunity to gain economic independence would benefit Beauvoir for the rest of her life.

In her early years of formal education, Beauvoir also developed significant relationships that yielded important insights for her. At age eight, she met her cousin Jacques Champigneulles and the two quickly bonded. They declared they were married (Beauvoir referred to him as her fiancé), but far from a mere childhood game, the two maintained an affectionate relationship for years to come. It was through her relationship with Jacques that Beauvoir realized not all men would treat her as an attractive object; he was attracted to her because of her mind. At the age of nine, Beauvoir formed an intimate friendship with Elizabeth Mabille, or Zaza. Beauvoir was enamored with Zaza who was defiant and sharp. The two would spend their childhood and adolescence together, confronting and resisting the rigid expectations of femininity imposed on their lives. This was harder for Zaza whose family expected her to become a wife. Beauvoir and Zaza were inseparable and their attachment to one another exceeded the conventions of friendship. Beauvoir describes loving Zaza intensely. It was through her relationship with Zaza that Beauvoir began to think about how an individual experiences herself in relation to another—how one is seen and whom one is taken to be by others. In 1929, when Beauvoir was 20, Zaza died unexpectedly of meningitis. This was a tragic and traumatic experience for Beauvoir, and she suffered an intense heartbreak. She fictionalized their intimacy and her heartbreak in the novel *Inseparable*, which she wrote in 1954 but was withheld from publication until 2020.

Initially devout in her faith, at age 14 Beauvoir began to question the existence of God, which was a pivotal moment in her life, propelling her further toward the study of philosophy. Although long supportive of her intellect, neither of Beauvoir's parents were pleased with her burgeoning interest. Françoise was worried her daughter would become morally corrupt and Georges thought philosophy was nonsense. Rather than seek the approval of her parents, Beauvoir chose philosophy. While the absence of a dowry made it easier for her to eschew the stifling expectations of heterosexual marriage and motherhood, this choice was definitely bold for her time. Philosophy was a man's domain. Nevertheless, in 1925, at the age of 17, Beauvoir passed the baccalaureate exams in mathematics and philosophy. In 1926, she earned Certificates of Higher Studies in French literature and Latin after studying at the Institut Catholique and the Institut Sainte-Marie. Beauvoir was not allowed to attend the most prestigious institution, the École Normale Supérieure, to study philosophy because she was a woman. So, in the fall of 1926, she began her studies at the Sorbonne. In 1928–1929 she wrote her graduate thesis on German mathematician and philosopher, Gottfried Wilhelm Leibniz, of which there is no surviving copy, prior to taking the competitive agrégation exam in philosophy in 1929. While Beauvoir was keen on pursuing her studies, she would also experience her education and academic success as a rupture in her life. She found great comfort in the intellectual life and the future it opened for her, but she also found it extremely lonely. Her studies prompted her to break away from the formative values of her upbringing and thus from her social class, leaving her to rethink and remake who she was and what values she lived by.

During the time Beauvoir was ascending the ranks of philosophy in France, the discipline was held in the highest regard. Those who could endure the rigorous examinations were understood to be the intellectual elite. Beauvoir passed the exam at 21, making her the eighth woman and youngest candidate to ever pass the agrégation. She finished in second place, behind Jean-Paul Sartre who had taken the exam for the second time. Her success on the exam interested another soon-to-be famous French philosopher, Maurice Merleau-Ponty, and the two quickly became dear friends. In the second volume of her autobiography, *The Prime of Life*, Beauvoir recounts this time in her life as carefree. Unlike the attitude she would adopt years later, she experienced herself as unencumbered by the world around her.

While studying for the agrégation, Beauvoir and Sartre found in each other intellectual companions and lovers, forming an unorthodox and controversial relationship. In October of 1929, when Beauvoir was 21 and Sartre 24, the two sat outside of the Louvre in Paris and made a now famous pact, one that for the longest time was often given more attention than Beauvoir's own work. They declared themselves "essential lovers," allowing for "contingent loves" that they disclosed to one another. This open relationship was radical for the time, especially for a woman. The two would never marry, would never live together, and pursued romantic and sexual relationships individually. Beauvoir would go on to have numerous relationships with men and women, but none paralleled the one with American author Nelson Algren, whom she fell deeply in love with. In various personal writings and the publication of their love letters in *A Transatlantic Love Affair: Letters to Nelson Algren*, Beauvoir's love for Algren was profound, likely a different kind of love than what she experienced with Sartre. In fact, when she was buried alongside Sartre in the Montparnasse Cemetery in Paris, she was wearing the ring Nelson Algren had given her many years earlier.

Her love relationships were not definitive of her existence, but they animate philosophical issues that preoccupied Beauvoir: the role of love in life and the ethical bond between self and other that takes shape in an erotic encounter. She would consider these issues across many of her literary and philosophical works. Yet, Beauvoir did not elevate her experience as an ethical ideal. She recognized her relationship with Sartre was not easy, she struggled with jealousy, and, in written correspondence with Sartre, she acknowledged she/they had caused others to suffer. And, others have more heavily criticized their questionable engagements with students, Olga Kosakiewicz and Bianca Bienenfield. Although, as Kate Kirkpatrick (2019) richly illustrates in her biography of Beauvoir, it is impossible to know exactly what happened in each of these relationships, there is no doubt that these relationships were complicated, and Beauvoir was far from perfect. What is certain is that when Olga and Bianca were in the picture, Beauvoir did not tell the truth about her concurrent relationships. As Kirkpatrick writes, "Beauvoir's concealed relationships with [Jacques] Bost, Olga, and Bianca reveal ... a disturbing willingness to deceive others—in particular, other women. In the case of Bost, her relationship with him revealed her complicity in the life-long deception of a woman she called her friend" (2019, 154).

As we will come to see, this aspect of Beauvoir's personal life contradicts her own commitments to ethical bonds with others. At the same time, Beauvoir was interested in thinking through the complexities, and multiple, often conflicting, meanings at work in experiences with others, and it is *from* the experience of life (and love) that Beauvoir pursued her thinking. For instance, her first novel, *She Came to Stay*, written in 1940 and published in 1943, Beauvoir fictionalizes the triadic relationship between herself, Sartre, and Olga Kosakiewic, a student of the two philosophers.

The pact between Sartre and Beauvoir itself defied convention, but the way their relationship shaped Beauvoir's life followed a very expected gendered narrative. Beauvoir was often defined exclusively in relation to Sartre, whereas he was viewed as an individual. He was considered an original philosopher; she was his follower. Even when Sartre would credit Beauvoir for *her* impact on his work, publicly it had little uptake. Although Beauvoir herself did little to challenge such a depiction publicly, her diaries and memoirs tell another story. Many of Beauvoir's philosophical ideas were in development before she met Sartre and many of her ideas are quite distinct from his, if only one were to study them.

It is, however, unsurprising that it is often difficult to think about Beauvoir's life without Sartre. Much of her formative young adult and intellectual years involved her relationship with him. After she concluded her tenure as the first woman to teach philosophy in a Parisian boys' school in 1929, she took a teaching position in Marseille, a city in southern France, moving away from Sartre. Her position was at an all-girls school where she challenged her students to engage in liberal thinking about labor and justice. Without the distraction of Sartre or Paris, Marseille allowed Beauvoir the time to start writing again. She also spent more time outdoors, often walking and hiking for hours a day, activities Sartre had no interest in. But, in 1932, she was assigned a teaching position in Rouen, in northern France, only 90 kilometers away from Sartre who was in Le Havre. At this time, she and Sartre visited one another frequently. They would travel and go on dates together, and they also began to research, write, and develop ideas alongside one another.

As Beauvoir's teaching career and romantic and intellectual companionship with Sartre progressed, Hitler was rising to power. Beauvoir did not yet have a political consciousness, though. Her concerns were with her inner life, rather than the public world around her. She and Sartre, still unknown to the world, continued to travel all over, on their teaching breaks, taking advantage of their independence and privilege as rising unemployment and xenophobia came to characterize the economic and political situation. At the end of the 1930s, when Beauvoir had already returned to Paris to teach, France declared war on Germany. Beauvoir saw men she loved, including Sartre, become enlisted and witnessed the swift occupation of France by the Nazis. By 1941, she was dismissed from her teaching post, which would later be reinstated in 1945 but Beauvoir would never teach again.

The Nazi Occupation and the changing social and political climate of WWII, as well as changes in her personal life, had a profound impact on Beauvoir. During this time, she abandoned the rationalist-voluntarist position of her youth, and she abandoned the primarily metaphysical focus on the self and other that defined her earlier years. She became more preoccupied with political and moral questions and thinking about the concreteness of social context. She would later call this time the "moral period" of her work. In the early 1940s, she participated in war resistance efforts, while also financially supporting her mother after the death of her father in 1941. The loss of her teaching post also allowed her to focus on her writing.

From 1941–1949, Beauvoir began to write and publish prolifically. In 1944, one year after the publication of *She Came to Stay*, she authored and published her first philosophical essay "Pyrrhus et Cineas." The novel, *The Blood of Others*, written in the Café de Flore in Paris, which examines the issues of freedom and responsibility through the lives of Parisians during and after the war, was published in 1945. That same year, she helped found the leftist journal *Les Temps Modernes* with other French intellectuals, including Sartre and Merleau-Ponty. Beauvoir was a co-editor of the journal, and it quickly became an important venue for philosophical and political essays of the time, including Beauvoir's essay "Eye for an Eye," which was inspired by and written during the trial and execution of a French intellectual who corroborated with the Nazis. It was also in 1945 that Beauvoir, along with Sartre, became well known in the public eye and was increasingly identified as an existentialist. In 1946, Beauvoir published another novel, *All Men Are Mortal*, and in 1947, *The Ethics of Ambiguity* was published, one of her more well-known philosophical manuscripts. Beginning in January 1947, Beauvoir traveled to and across the United States for four months on a lecture tour sponsored by the French government. On this trip, she met Nelson Algren and authored her first "travel writing," *America Day by Day*, which offers reflections on American capitalism, racism, and sexism.

Not too long after, Beauvoir began publishing excerpts of what would become *The Second Sex* in *Les Temps Modernes*.

The publication of *The Second Sex* in 1949 would launch Beauvoir further into the public spotlight. It neither immediately defined her career nor was it the only peak of her career—the esteemed, award-winning novel *The Mandarins* was published in 1954. But, *The Second Sex* undoubtedly marked a change in her thinking and activism, as well as propelled her toward a notable place in feminist history. While in the early 1930s Beauvoir would not dare call herself a feminist, when *The Second Sex* was published, at the age of 41, Beauvoir had undeniably developed a feminist consciousness. She had, like the other women around her, become aware that she had been defined and confined in her sex. Her feminist perspective did not necessarily mark a drastic change in her philosophical concerns. Rather, her focus became more concrete, more attentive to how particular realities, like being a woman, changed the meaning and experience of existence. Her work on aging, *The Coming of Age*, published in 1970, is a clear continuation of such work. Initially prompted by her involvement in resistance efforts, it was really with and after the publication of *The Second Sex* that Beauvoir understood her pen to be a means for social and political change.

In the later years of her life, Beauvoir continued her political activism and secured for herself a place in twentieth-century intellectual history. As will be discussed in detail in Chapter 7, in contrast to her earlier years, Beauvoir had crafted a deeply political life, one in which she took strong feminist, socialist, and anti-colonial positions, and stood against all forms of oppression. She also continued to think and write about the issues that had long concerned her: bourgeois ideals, the relation between the self and others, love, embodiment, freedom, and responsibility. In doing so, she secured a place in philosophical and literary history. She also endured the death of her mother and Sartre, both of which she would write about as significant experiences of loss. Although it was not until decades later that Beauvoir's intellectual legacy would receive the full recognition it deserved, when Beauvoir died, there was still public mourning in her honor. She was deemed an "authentic heroine."

There is no doubt that Beauvoir's life was epic. This fact is not because Beauvoir was destined to be who she became. Her own philosophical commitments deny the idea that there is an inner, predetermined essence, a being, to who we are. The classic philosophical distinction between **being** and **becoming**, between an internal, unchanging essence and an always-changing, shifting of existence, is clearly disclosed in the unfolding of Beauvoir's life. After spending the latter half of her life as a feminist icon, public intellectual, and eminent writer, Beauvoir died at 78, on April 14, 1986. She is buried, with Sartre, in the Montparnasse Cemetery in Paris.

INFLUENCES

Far from being a devout disciple of a particular thinker or philosophical tradition, Beauvoir's work evinces the influence of numerous philosophical traditions, philosophers, and writers, as well as styles. The result is the ability to see in Beauvoir's work concerns and approaches that are characteristic of specific traditions and to see innovation in style and method that is identifiably Beauvoirian. Her influences were not merely intellectual or generated solely from strict academic sources, formal education, or a strict adherence to the discipline of philosophy. Beauvoir's work was also informed by her upbringing and formative relationships, authors and poets, and the social and political events of her time. Insofar as the question of influence is itself a philosophical one—what does it mean to be influenced? What are the criteria that demarcate influence?—the following offers a sketch of the thinkers and events often understood to have significantly influenced Beauvoir, with the admission that the traces of influence in her work are eclectic and abundant.

As a young teen, Beauvoir took an interest in philosophy. It was an antidote to the dreary dogmatism of her Catholic upbringing. In philosophy, she found not simply a discipline that asked questions, but one that asked them of her, of her life and self. During these early years of her philosophical training, Beauvoir studied logic, moral philosophy, and metaphysics, as well as psychology and mathematics. She studied canonical thinkers like St. Thomas Aquinas and Plato, and she came to appreciate philosophical doubt as a generative mode of thinking. This appreciation would lead her to secular thinking and eventually to atheism, a defining feature of her later existentialist commitments.

As was the standard in France, Beauvoir's training was extremely demanding and involved a rigorous engagement with the history of Western philosophy and required a breadth of knowledge across the discipline. She studied at length the works of René Descartes, Baruch Spinoza, Immanuel Kant, Jean Jacques Rousseau, Alfred Fouillée, Arthur Schopenhauer, Friedrich Nietzsche, and Henri Bergson, among many, many others. She, like other young, radical scholars in the late 1920s, also sought out thinkers excluded from the syllabi of her courses, including G.W.F. Hegel, who she would return to later in the late 1930s and early 1940s. At the end of her education, for the agrégation exam, she wrote on the theme of "Freedom and Contingency," which would remain a key theme in her future work.

Near the end of Beauvoir's education and early into the 1930s, around Beauvoir's mid-20s, her intellectual influences broadened. Another burgeoning philosopher, Raymond Aron encouraged her and Sartre to read German phenomenology and the work of Edmund Husserl in particular. At that point, both Beauvoir and Sartre had read a little bit of Martin Heidegger's work, Husserl's student and former assistant, and Beauvoir had likely read some Husserl while she studied under her teacher Jean Baruzi, but neither had set out on a focused study of German phenomenology. While Beauvoir describes Sartre as more quickly moved to take up the study of phenomenology, it is evident it was influential to them both. Beauvoir and Sartre, as well as Merleau-Ponty, studied Husserl and Heidegger, and Emmanuel Levinas, another student of Husserl's.

Beauvoir saw in phenomenology a method of philosophy that would allow her to tend to first-person lived experience. Most of the thinkers she encountered throughout her training had made philosophy too abstract, too oriented toward systematic thinking. Phenomenology offered her an alternative. For Husserl, **phenomenology** is a study of phenomena or "things" as they appear in first-person, conscious experience, that is, **lived experience** (*Erlebnis*). Like Descartes, who saw the individual subject as the point of departure for philosophical inquiry, phenomenology starts from an individual's lived experience of a phenomenon. The phenomenological method, a *way of doing* philosophical inquiry, is captured in Husserl's dictum: "Back to the things themselves!" The task of the phenomenologist is to describe the various ways a particular phenomenon, a specific "thing," is given in the world and how it is consciously experienced by those to whom it appears. For Husserl, the descriptive method should bracket or put out of play what Husserl calls the **natural attitude**, the everyday, taken-for-granted experience and understanding of a given phenomenon. In doing so, a phenomenological description discloses the essential structures of the experience. It generates an understanding of the phenomenon under investigation that *transcends* the empirical world, giving a *pure description* of the intrinsic conditions of its appearance.

Beauvoir would ultimately reject Husserl's transcendental phenomenology, seeing it as too abstract and universalizing. Nevertheless, she was drawn to the promise of the method of phenomenological inquiry, and she adapted Husserl and Heidegger for her own aims. In Heidegger, Beauvoir found an understanding of human existence as both individual and sociohistorical, or an ontology (the study of being) wherein the world and being are entangled. Beauvoir's engagement with phenomenology also brought her to center a concern with the body, which she shared with her friend and intellectual peer, Merleau-Ponty. Merleau-Ponty credits Beauvoir and her first published novel, *She Came to Stay*, with inspiring his own thinking on embodiment, as well as on temporality, and Beauvoir was surely influenced by Merleau-Ponty's development of a phenomenology of embodiment in his work, *Phenomenology of Perception*. They both took to and reworked Husserl's notion of the **lived body** (Leib), which refers not to the physiological, biological body, but to subjectivity, the *me* that comes into being, as lived *in* and *as* a bodily existence. In other words, rather than understanding experience to be formed purely by the mind or conscious thought, Beauvoir understands experience as an embodied constitution. The body-subject is the locus of/for lived experience. In *The Second Sex* Beauvoir accounts for the lived body in the following way: "It is not the body-object described by the biologist that actually exists, but the body as lived [le corps veçu] by the subject." The significance of the phenomenological concepts of lived experience and lived body are central to many of her works and they are formative to her notion of **situation**, which is discussed in detail in the next chapter.

By the early 1940s, Hegel was also a key figure in Beauvoir's thinking. While working on her first novel, *She Came to Stay*, she would spend days on end in the Bibliothèque Nationale in Paris reading his work, especially Hegel's *Phenomenology of Spirit*. She was so influenced by this book that *She Came to Stay* begins with an epigraph from it. Like most French intellectuals of her time, Beauvoir's understanding of Hegel was largely, but not solely, informed by Alexandre Kojève's interpretation. Kojève, who brought Hegel into twentieth-century French philosophy, offers an interpretation of Hegel influenced by Karl Marx and Heidegger. Kojève focuses on Hegel's master-slave dialectic, a forced relation of recognition, to think about self-consciousness, subordination, and freedom. As with most of the thinkers that were formative to Beauvoir's work, she did not merely take Hegel at his word. She rejected the systematic tendencies in Hegel's thinking, but she took to his relational understanding of the self, his account of the struggle for recognition, and his theory of mutual recognition. Indeed, her account of women's existence in *The Second Sex* where her key claim that woman is the Other is unequivocally inspired by Hegel's master-slave dialectic.

Yet, as Beauvoir writes in her *Wartime Diary* ([1990] 2009), she turned to Danish philosopher, Søren Kierkegaard, often regarded as the father of existentialism, to save herself from what she calls Hegel's rationalist optimism. Beauvoir was acquainted with Kierkegaard from previous studies, but it was not until 1939 that she turned to him for inspiration. His thinking, and his existentialist ethics in particular, would play an important role in her reckoning with the Nazi Occupation of Paris and the aftermath of the war. In the post-war period, Beauvoir grappled with atrocities that had become commonplace and deciding *how to live* knowing the violence and evil that could be done by choice, even if out of complicity, was at the forefront for Beauvoir. In Kierkegaard, she found a way to think about subjectivity as active and chosen, which challenged views of human nature that understand the self to be predetermined. Kierkegaard offered a way to think about lived, individual becoming, which gave Beauvoir a way to address how, especially in the face of dark times and collective despair, it is possible to not resign to complicity, and how an individual can live their life in resistance. Beauvoir came to draw on Kierkegaard in numerous works, converting his religious existentialist insights to develop her secular existentialist morality (she found inspiration in Nietzsche's atheism for the latter). Kierkegaard's influence is pronounced in her novels *The Blood of Others* and *The Mandarins*, and in her account of women's liberation in *The Second Sex*.

In the 1940s, Beauvoir would become increasingly influenced by Karl Marx. She had long believed capitalism to be exploitative and oppressive but never committed herself to Marxism. She rejected the deterministic and reductionist aspects of his thinking, believing that it allowed individuals to deny responsibility for historical events. She was drawn to his insights about class exploitation, labor as constitutive of an individual's existence, and his insistence that the aim of the struggle for liberation should be to make existence less alienated, and so more fully human. Like many of her influences, citations to Marx can be found throughout her work, from *The Ethics of Ambiguity* all the way to the 1970 publication of *The Coming of Age*.

It is important to emphasize that Beauvoir had additional influences. Bergson's considerations of time and free choice and Fouillée's claim, "Man is not born, but rather becomes, free," all played an important role in shaping Beauvoir's thinking. In the realm of literature, she drew motivation and influence in style, technique, and concerns from various authors, including French authors Maurice Barrès and André Gide, British authors Virginia Woolf and George Eliot, and American authors William Faulkner, Ernest Hemingway, and Richard Wright. She often undertook extensive interdisciplinary research, reading widely in fields like economics, history, sociology, psychology, and psychoanalysis. Such an approach was key to *The Second Sex*, *The Long March*, and *The Coming of Age*. Beauvoir was also taken by Gunnar Myrdal's 1944 sociological study of American race relations in *An American Dilemma*, which played an important role in her theorizations of racial oppression in *America Day by Day*.

FORM AND METHODS

The result of these varying and widespread influences is a thinker who is neither pure philosopher nor pure author. Her concepts, styles, and methods are the result of a process of conversion, borrowing from, finding ideas in, and working with various thinkers. Since she had rejected abstract and systematic philosophizing early in her studies, she aimed to do philosophy in a way that did not impose meaning, declare an absolute truth, or establish a rigid, moral doctrine. The philosophical essay's move to universalize bothered her; she saw it as obscuring subjective, first-person experience.

As a result, Beauvoir was keener on using literary forms and she regularly called herself an author, not a philosopher. She used various literary genres, including autobiography and travel writing, but she understood the novel as the best genre for phenomenological description. In her essay, "Literature and Metaphysics," Beauvoir describes being torn between the "concrete, temporal world" of fiction and the abstract mode of philosophical inquiry that carried her "beyond the terrestrial appearances into the serenity of a timeless heaven" ([1946] 2004, 269). For her, the novel offered a way to reckon with the concrete, reconstituting "on an imaginary plane this experience itself as it appears prior to any elucidation," such that the task of the novel is "evoke this flesh-and-blood presence whose complexity and singular and infinite richness exceed any subjective interpretation" (270). In other words, the task of the novelist is to disclose the multiple meanings, experiences, and complexities of the concrete, historical world without resolving them through the sense-making practice of philosophical inquiry. Through the novel, "[t]he reader ponders, doubts, and takes sides; and this hesitant development of his thought enriches him in a way that no teaching of doctrine could" (270). This view of fiction and the novel, as well as her admitted love for both literature and philosophy, is what led her to develop the articulate an account of the **metaphysical novel**. Distinct from literary fiction that advances and defends a thesis (a *roman à thèse*), the *metaphysical novel* is a form and style that reveals the contingency of the world, along with its multiple, interwoven meanings, bringing to light contradictions of circumstance and in human choices. She saw literature as a way to overcome the existential separation between self and other, to engage and be undone by other truths. The result is literature with ethical and political implications and Beauvoir harnessed it to make overt leftist critiques of social conventions and bourgeois ideology.

"Well-made plots always irritated me by their artificiality," Beauvoir writes in *Force of Circumstance*, the third volume of her autobiography (([1963] 1992a, 249). "I wanted to imitate the disorder, the indecision, the contingency of life." Accordingly, her novels disclose some of her own ethical concerns and positions that emerged in and from her own lived experience, recreated and fictionalized. It is thus best to understand Beauvoir's body of work as literary *and* philosophical. She makes use of literature to do philosophy, to investigate the world and lived experience, and she also draws on literature to inform her works that more closely approximate the conventions of philosophical texts.

As Beauvoir studied Husserl, Heidegger, and Kierkegaard, and conversed with Sartre during and after WWII, the two began to focus on a distinct set of philosophical problems and developed ideas that would become identifiable as **existentialism**, a term coined by French philosopher, Gabriel Marcel. Even as existentialist thought can be traced back to Kierkegaard, Nietzsche, and Heidegger, the popularization of the moniker "existentialist" became apparent in the post-war climate. Intellectuals and the public were looking for ways to grapple with how to exist in the world as they now saw it, as dark, violent, and unjust. They were also trying to make sense of the complicity with the Holocaust, as well as the moral value of resistance. As a result, in 1945, Beauvoir and Sartre entered the spotlight. In that year, which Beauvoir refers to as the "existentialist offensive," she published her second novel,

The Blood of Others, the leftist journal *Les Temps Modernes*, founded by Beauvoir, Sartre, and Merleau-Ponty, was launched, and Sartre had published several key works.

It was also the year that Beauvoir and Sartre also went public with their respective work. On October 29, 1945, Beauvoir's first and only play *Useless Mouths* had its opening performance and Sartre gave his famous lecture-turned book, *Existentialism is a Humanism*. At his lecture, often hailed as a defining moment in twentieth-century existentialist philosophy, Sartre coined the phrase, "existence precedes essence," capturing a key existentialist commitment. This assertion means there is no essence to being human, there is no such thing as a predetermined human nature because what it is to be human is made and decided through existing. In other words, the me that I am, or the you that you are, is not predetermined by nature or by God, but by what we make of ourselves. For Beauvoir, it is also a matter of the social constraints around us and who we are able to become as a result. This commitment should not, however, be equated with a response to the nature-nurture question or with a tenet of social constructionism that says we are merely constructed by society or culture. Rather, the existentialist claim is that what it means to be a subject, to be a "me" or a "you," is a matter of becoming not being. While Beauvoir's play was not received with the acclaim of Sartre's lecture, *Useless Mouths* also highlights key existentialist themes, including our capacity to choose injustice or freedom in the face of violence and domineering power in the present. *The Blood of Others* takes up similar themes, grappling with the issues of freedom and responsibility in the context of war. These works highlight that Beauvoir's existentialism deals with the moral problems that arise in the concrete world in which one lives. As she saw it, existentialism is a philosophy with political implications. It is not a coincidence, then, that Beauvoir's "moral period" is bound up with her becoming an existentialist.

While some scholars see Beauvoir as deploying the traditional phenomenological method of Husserl, many others insist that, in the development of Beauvoir's thinking, she transformed the phenomenological method. Pointing to *The Second Sex* as an innovation in the phenomenological method for the way

Beauvoir attends to the meaning of "woman," other scholars regard Beauvoir as the founding mother of **feminist phenomenology**, a kind of critical phenomenology that seeks to describe *and* change the world. A traditional or classical phenomenological investigation aims for *pure description*, one that reflects on and describes the transcendental structures, or the essential structures, of conscious, first-person experience, and it deploys the phenomenological epoché (a "suspension of judgment") to bracket the prejudicial natural attitude. This bracketing allows the phenomenologist to uncover what is prior to the contingent structures, the ones dependent on social and historical context. Beauvoir, however, rejects the idea that there are structures that precede the social and historical and does not presume that the phenomenologist can bracket out her own preconceptions. Rather, she goes right into them and investigates contingencies, refusing the idea that there is anything "prior to" or essential to grasp. Her phenomenological investigation addresses the experiences of numerous others, showing that there is no singular, governing perspective, and takes seriously how injustice and subordination are themselves constitutive structures of experience, not mere overlays of the empirical world.

Although there are precursors in her novels, it is arguably in *The Second Sex* that Beauvoir *shows* us her feminist phenomenological method most explicitly. In this work, she *does* a feminist phenomenology of sexual difference, investigating the phenomenon of "woman" and what it means to be one. Whereas in her earlier philosophical text, *The Ethics of Ambiguity*, Beauvoir would criticize her thinking for remaining abstract, in *The Second Sex* Beauvoir commits to the concrete, focusing on how contingent structures have been rendered essential, made to seem *as if* they are transcendental, through human choice and action. She narrates, at length, historically sedimented and value-laden meanings of "woman," as well as the economic structures that condition its possibility, dedicating almost a thousand pages to work through numerous sources to lay bare the particularity of the phenomenon, that is, to show how "woman" appears in the concreteness of various first-person perspectives. In working at the level of the contingent Beauvoir also shows us the generality of the phenomenon, or what tracks across perspectives. By staying within the social world, Beauvoir eschews the masculinist tradition to seek universality. For this reason, her phenomenological practice is a feminist one not only because she is the first to offer a feminist phenomenological account of sexed embodiment, but also because she tends to the entanglement of the general and the particular, exposing the masculinist myth of generic experience.

Beauvoir later develops this phenomenological practice in *The Coming of Age*. In this book, she describes how the universal human experience of aging is never experienced in its universality. Rather, it is an experience structured and conditioned by a particular situation, that is, a specific social, historical, economic, and political context. As such, aging is always experienced in its particularity, even as there are shared, general features of aging by those living in a similar situation. Ultimately, she shows us that one cannot think about the reality of sexual difference or old age in an abstract, universal way. These phenomena do not exist prior to contingency but are rendered essential through sociohistorical.

Her phenomenological practice, the way she *does* phenomenology, aims to transform the phenomenon she describes. In doing so, Beauvoir politicizes phenomenology. In *The Second Sex* Beauvoir uncovers the injustice of what it means to exist as a woman. In her description of this subordinated existence, she exposes how patriarchal structures that condition the visceral, lived experience of women are the effects of human choices and values, even if those choices and values are not always consciously undertaken. It is in this exposure that her existentialist ethics enter the scene. The description puts the injustice women experience in our faces and we become morally burdened with the choice to live differently. *The Coming of Age* also exposes injustice, and Beauvoir labors to bring us to a place where we are moved by the reality to think, act, create values, and ultimately live in a different way. Of course, she knows there is no guarantee that we will. She knows we could take comfort in the status quo of injustice or seek false solutions in abstract moral systems. But, for her, it is our freedom of choice to remain complicit or to assume our lives in ways that open freedom for ourselves and others.

Since at least the early 1920s, Beauvoir had a clear interest in the philosophical problem of **intersubjectivity**, or the relation and opposition between self and other(s). Inspired by the texts and thinkers she read, as well as her own experience, this interest is described in her earliest diaries, present in her very first novel, and remains central in her final works. The methods she employed to think about intersubjectivity aim to bring to light the ambiguities of lived, embodied experience, including the moral dilemmas that arise for us, as we live our lives. Ultimately, over the course of her life and work, she refined her intellectual practice, making out of philosophy *and* literature a way to grapple with and be affected by the world we live in and share with others.

WHY READ BEAUVOIR?

Studying the life and work of Simone de Beauvoir can help us think about who we are and how we ought to live. As you will see throughout this book, her work challenges us to rethink what we know about ourselves, about the world around us, and about how to live. She insists that we can and must take responsibility for the world we were thrown into and the choices we make or don't make. This responsibility entails a specific ethical demand for Beauvoir: we must open freedom for ourselves and others. The demand is not a simple one; time and time again, she tells us, we are faced with or constrained by our situation in ways that entice us to choose freedom for ourselves but not others, or that have already cast a limit on freedom. Beauvoir's insistence is that philosophy should bring us right into that situation to show us that we have the capacity to change, to create, and to imagine new ways of existing.

Yet, we also are not the sole authors of our own lives. For Beauvoir, we are shaped by circumstance, the actions of others, and constituted and constrained by factors we did not make or choose, including the reality of our own body. Our very existence, the self we each become, and the lives we each live, are not, then, individually made. This understanding of the self and life are central to all of Beauvoir's work, but they are nowhere more apparent than in her numerous diaries and her multi-volume autobiography that recounts 54 years of her life from 1908–1962. These life writings are an investigation of her self, offering not a mere chronology, but a narrative about how events and experiences, and relations with others are how we become who we are. While Beauvoir is deliberate in her narration, disclosing only what she chooses, these writings offer a philosophy of self that insists we are neither isolated entities with sovereign rule over ourselves nor are we objects moved by an external force. We are who we are because of how we assume our existence in relation to others in the world and the circumstances we are in. Even if we have not reckoned with this reality, Beauvoir would insist this is true for each of us. In reading her work, we might begin to grapple more with who we are now and who we could become.

Her life, her writings, and her political efforts show us that *we become who we are*, and not just one time, but several times over again. We may have one life, but we live many selves. Who others expect us to be is not who we have to become. Yet, for Beauvoir, who we become is not a matter of pure choice or radical freedom. We are shaped and changed by the circumstances around us and how we do and can assume and negotiate them. Beauvoir is no exception. The circumstances of her life and the way she wrestled and struggled with them, as well as her own individual challenges to the societal expectations that had been laid out for her, were generative of her original ideas and formative to her political activism. They were also generative of her own project to live a life that affirms freedom in the face of constraint. As Alice Schwarzer, writes, "Simone de Beauvoir herself, her life and her work, was—and is—a symbol; a symbol of possibility, despite everything, of living one's life the way one wants to, for oneself, free from conventions and prejudices, even as a woman" (1984, 13).

SUGGESTED READING

Primary Texts

Beauvoir, Simone de. [1958] 1959. *Memoirs of a Dutiful Daughter*. Translated by James Kirkup. Cleveland: World Publishing.

—— [1960] 1962. *The Prime of Life: The Autobiography of Simone de Beauvoir*. Translated by Peter Green. Cleveland: World Publishing.

—— [1963] 1992. *The Force of Circumstance, I: The Autobiography of Simone de Beauvoir 1944–1952*. Translated by Richard Howard. New York: Paragon House.

—— [1963] 1992. *The Force of Circumstance, II: The Autobiography of Simone de Beauvoir 1952–1962*. Translated by Richard Howard. New York: Paragon House.

—— [1972] 1993. *All Said and Done: The Autobiography of Simone de Beauvoir 1962–1972*. Translated by Patrick O'Brian. New York: Paragon House.

—— 2006. *Diary of a Philosophy Student: Volume 1, 1926–27*. Translated by Barbara Klaw, edited by Sylvie Le Bon de Beauvoir, Margaret A. Simons, and Marybeth Timmerman. Urbana: University of Illinois Press.

—— [1990] 2009. *Wartime Diary*. Translated by Anne Deing Cordero, edited by Sylvie Le Bon de Beauvoir, and Margaret A. Simons. Urbana: University of Illinois Press.

—— 2019. *Diary of a Philosophy Student: Volume 2, 1928–29*. Translated by Barbara Klaw, edited by Sylvie Le Bon de Beauvoir, Margaret A. Simons, and Marybeth Timmerman. Urbana: University of Illinois Press.

—— 2024. *Diary of a Philosophy Student: Volume 3, 1926–30*. Translated by Barbara Klaw, edited by Sylvie Le Bon de Beauvoir and Margaret A. Simons. Urbana: University of Illinois Press.

Secondary Texts

Bair, Deidre. 1990. *Simone de Beauvoir: A Biography*. New York: Summit Books.

Daigle, Christine and Jacob Golomb, eds. 2009. *Beauvoir and Sartre: The Riddle of Influence*, Bloomington: Indiana University Press.

Fallaize, Elizabeth, ed. 1998. *Simone de Beauvoir: A Critical Reader*. London: Routledge.

Kirkpatrick, Kate, 2019. *Becoming Beauvoir: A Life*. London: Bloomsbury.

Moi, Toril. 2008. *The Making of an Intellectual Woman*, Second Edition. Oxford: Oxford University Press.

Tidd, Ursula. 1999. *Simone de Beauvoir Gender and Testimony*. Cambridge: Cambridge University Press.

2

WHAT IS FREEDOM?

In the spring of 1939 Beauvoir had a profound realization that others played a constitutive role in her existence. In many ways, this realization was due to the reality of World War II. The moral and political questions the war threw into sharp relief led Beauvoir to reject the solipsism that had previously character-ized her life and thinking. By the 1940s, Beauvoir did not take the individual self to be the whole of reality and she rejected the view that there is, as a matter of metaphysical truth, a fun-damental conflict between self and other. Despite rejecting such a truth, she examines such conflict in her first novel, *She Came to Stay*, which was published in 1943. In this novel, Beauvoir depicts the "alien consciousness" of the other as a fundamental threat to the self. In her subsequent works, she changed course, understanding the opposition between self and other to be gen-erated by social and political circumstances. Far from being an inherent truth about human nature, Beauvoir came to see that conflicts between people are made and shaped by human choices and actions. So, while *She Came to Stay* undoubtedly examines the ethics of our relationships with others, it is from 1943 onwards that Beauvoir's ethical work takes a committed political stance. This shift in her thinking inaugurated what she refers to as "the moral period" of her career.

Central to Beauvoir's moral period is the development of her existential phenomenological conception of freedom. In large part, the existential tradition accounts for **ontological freedom**, describing freedom as a fundamental category of "the human" and definitive of human existence. From an existentialist

DOI: 10.4324/9781003399995-2

viewpoint, we are self-conscious beings who exist for ourselves, defined by our capacity to be self-aware and purposeful. That is, we are free existents who create who and how we are through the choices and actions we undertake. Accordingly, we are neither determined by God or biology nor are we mere effects of our environment. We are not naturally destined to be anything at all. Rather, existentialism posits that we are condemned to freedom, burdened, and often anguished, by the reality that who we become, individually and collectively, is on us. For an existentialist like Beauvoir, it is human actions and choices that make the world and constitute the lives we live.

Although Beauvoir agrees with the tenet of ontological freedom, she carves out another way to understand freedom. In the early 1940s, through her critical engagement with Sartre's ontological account of freedom in *Being and Nothingness*, Beauvoir begins to develop an account of **moral freedom**. For Beauvoir, moral freedom is a matter of how we assume our existence in relation to others. A genuinely free existence, she insists, requires and relies on the pursuit and realization of ethical bonds with others. So, while we are free in the sense that our existence has no metaphysical essence, Beauvoir wants us to understand and assume our freedom in ways that affirm not only our own freedom but the freedom of others.

Beauvoir's conception of moral freedom is one of her key contributions to existentialist ethics. For Beauvoir, even if human beings are free in the ontological sense, it does not mean that we are free in the moral sense. Moral freedom is the kind of freedom that we must struggle to realize, and we do so, she argues, by considering how our actions impact the freedom of others. Accordingly, the realization of an individual's moral freedom is dependent on their existence in relation to others. For Beauvoir, the self-other relation, or **intersubjectivity**, is a fundamental dimension of individual existence. In other words, the self that I am is always in relation to you, the other. This reality raises important questions: What is my relation to the other? How should I live with the other? As this chapter explains in detail, Beauvoir's theory of moral freedom insists that for an individual to be genuinely free, they must promote the freedom of others. In the development of her conception of moral freedom, both in her works and as she lives it, she makes clear that realizing moral freedom requires a political commitment to end oppression.

In contrast to a liberal conception of the free, unbounded subject and a libertarian conception of political freedom wherein individual autonomy must be maximized, Beauvoir's existential account of freedom commits us to our relations with others, which demands limits on individual freedom. For her, to pursue moral freedom is not to do whatever one wants; it is to prioritize the relational dimension of our existence. This prioritization of our bond with others is a hallmark of Beauvoir's thinking. Her account of freedom helps shed light on the relationship between freedom and responsibility and challenges us to think about what it looks like to concretely strive to realize freedom *with* others, not just for ourselves.

EXISTENTIAL HUMANISM

Existentialism, the tradition of philosophy that Beauvoir is a part of, takes the human subject as its point of departure. It considers what is characteristic of human beings, positing that our capacity for freedom is a distinguishing feature of being human. Beauvoir is no different in this regard. She insists that because we are free beings, we should be able to create our own lives and the meaning of our existence. From this starting point, Beauvoir's work is defined by a concern for the meaning and conditions of freedom and grappling with the experiences that compromise freedom. However, it wasn't until the early 1940s, as Beauvoir developed her existential account of freedom, that she took up a tangible relation to humanism. As she did, she came to develop an existential humanism, one that discusses and reveals what prevents the whole of humanity from flourishing. For an existentialist like Beauvoir, we pursue our capacity for freedom through **projects**, or the world-building activity and commitments we actively take up and that are constitutive of and an articulation of who we each are. That is, projects are the way we give meaning to our lives, they disclose our values and commitments, and they create and affirm our individual and collective relation to the future. For Beauvoir, acting for the sake of the self-other relation, not just for ourselves, should be the aim of our projects.

Beauvoir's existentialism inherits Immanuel Kant's secular humanism, which anchors morality in human rationality or rational will. However, her secular humanism is more attuned to human interdependencies and what she calls the force of circumstance (*la force des choses*) than is the Kantian tradition. For Beauvoir, the self is not an autonomous, unbounded, freely willing agent. Instead, she takes the situation of the concrete existing individual, enveloped in the world, as her point of departure. She underscores that we are always bound and constrained, dependent on others and shaped by the concrete circumstances of the world we have been thrown into, which are largely ones we did not choose and are not at will to change on our own. She recognizes that some human beings live *as if* they are sovereign, unbounded subjects, even though none of us are. As necessarily embedded in the world and inescapably related to others, what kinds of projects we undertake and can pursue is not up to us. Our projects and thus our lives are shaped and constrained in ways beyond our control.

The condition of our existence as always in the world with others does not determine who we are. Rather, in its concreteness and particularity, this condition constitutes the horizon of each subject's lived experience. We are situated existents, Beauvoir insists. We are enveloped by and inseparable from contingent sociohistorical events and conditions and relations with others. Our existence is, then, never outside or beyond the world. It is in **situation**. This phenomenological notion of situation refers to the entirety of the physiological, psychological, social, economic, political, and historical conditions in and through which a subject assumes her existence. In other words, the very body an individual has is their situation just as much as the entire material, sociohistorical scene in which they live their body is also their situation. Neither determine who a subject is, however. As opposed to merely having a body and being determined by the external world, for Beauvoir, a subject lives an embodied existence in a concrete place. Her account of old age illustrates this notion of situation well. While getting old is a physiological and psychological phenomenon, which does constitute one's situation as aged, old age is never only lived as a mere or brute biological fact. It is, rather, a "status imposed upon him [a subject] by the society to which he belongs" ([1970] 1972, 9). Beauvoir's insistence on the existential dimension of old age underscores that one's situation is constituted by the entanglement of the body and the world, as well as by how an individual negotiates their body-self in the world.

Insofar as no two individuals are the same, Beauvoir posits that one's situation is always specific. She makes this point in *The Ethics of Ambiguity* when she writes, "man is man only through situations whose singularity is precisely a universal fact" ([1947] 1976, 144). In other words, we live particular existences, not a universal human existence. This commitment to our particularity does not mean Beauvoir refuses generality. She believes it is possible, and perhaps at times politically necessary, to reckon with the dimensions of a situation that generates shared experience. Accordingly, her existential humanism commits her to an engagement with the concrete and particular, rather than the abstract and universal. "In order for this world to have any importance," Beauvoir writes in *The Ethics of Ambiguity*, "in order for our undertaking to have a meaning and to be worthy of sacrifices, we must affirm the concrete and particular thickness of this world and the individual reality of our projects and ourselves" (106).

Beauvoir's attention to situation leads her to develop a concrete, rather than abstract account of freedom. She insists that if we want to pursue and live out moral freedom, we must commit to thinking from, existing concretely in, and addressing our situation. So, while our ontological freedom may be infinite, our moral freedom is not. It is bound, finite, limited, and sometimes, for some groups, compromised by others. As she writes in her first philosophical essay "Pyrrhus and Cineas," man "is free but not in the sense of that abstract freedom expounded by the Stoics; he is free in situation" ([1944] 2004, 86). For her, the truth is that situation can undermine or promote one's freedom; freedom is not a given.

In centering our inseparability from the world and others, Beauvoir's conception of freedom offers an alternative to the priority given to autonomy in the history of Western philosophy. Similarly, her existential humanism also challenges the view of the human subject as a thinking being. From Aristotle to Descartes to Kant, the human subject is elevated to the status of pure mind or pure rationality. For Beauvoir, however, to be human is to be an **embodied consciousness**; it is to be neither pure mind or pure matter, but always both mind and body. As such, humans are always independent and dependent, free and constrained. Political philosopher and Beauvoir scholar Sonia Kruks puts it best when she writes,

> To be human, says Beauvoir, is not to discover that one is essentially mind, or reason, or rational will. It is to discover, rather, that one is a strange and ambiguous existence: a corporeal being whose actions are 'free' insofar as they are not strictly determined and yet who is always already shaped and constrained by what one is and by the world in which one finds oneself bodily situation.
>
> (Kruks 2012, 27)

That we our embodied subjects is definitive of what Beauvoir refers to as our ambiguous ontological condition. In *The Ethics of Ambiguity*, Beauvoir most clearly outlines her notion of existential **ambiguity**. Each human subject, Beauvoir argues, is "a sovereign and unique subject amidst a universe of objects" and "an object for others" ([1947] 1976, 7). Refusing to affirm either side of the mind-body and subject-object split, Beauvoir posits instead that our existence is ambiguous. The experience of being human is to experience oneself as "a pure internality against which no external power can take hold" *and* "as a thing crushed by the dark weight of other things" (7). Neither pure mind nor pure matter, neither radical freedom nor determined, we are a part of the material world and conscious of the world. For Beauvoir, the history of Western philosophy has tended to try to resolve or escape this ontological ambiguity, lapsing into either idealism or materialism, thus reducing human existence to mind or matter. In fact, she begins *The Ethics of Ambiguity* with this important critique, asserting: "As long as there have been men and they have lived, they have all felt the tragic ambiguity of their condition, but as long as there have been philosophers and they have thought, most of them have tried to mask it" (7). Consequently, she aims to expose the ontological condition of our existence, and to ground an ethics in it. She insists that living an ethical existence means assuming, not refusing our ambiguity. Like the failure of philosophers to affirm our ambiguity, Beauvoir argues that most of us seek to deny our ambiguity. We do so, she says, to cope with the weight of responsibility that comes with assuming our ambiguity.

In rooting an ethics in our ambiguity, Beauvoir insists that we must realize that who we are is not predetermined. For Beauvoir, moral views that claim humans are by nature sinful and so must obey God or that we are, by nature, inherently evil and self-interested, and so violence and domination are inevitable, are justifications we give to the very choices we make. These justifications let us off the hook; they are excuses that allow us to continue to eschew our responsibility for ourselves and the social, material, and political conditions of our existence. But for Beauvoir, if domination exists, it is not because humans are naturally inclined to establish hierarchies and subjugate others; it is because of the choices human beings have made. At the same time, she insists that we must realize that we are also not absolutely free, mortal gods ourselves. To do whatever we desire, to be egoists or nihilists, is also to excuse ourselves from living ethically in the world. Such positions allow us to eclipse the burden of responsibility. Accordingly, in the face of evil we cannot look to God or lapse into claims about human nature or throw our hands up as if no one and nothing else matters; we must realize that it is human choices alone which matter. She begins her novel, *The Blood of Others* ([1945] 1964), with an epigraph from Dostoevsky's *The Brothers Karamazov* that asserts this point: "Each of us is responsible for everything and to every human being."

When we admit and assume our ambiguity, we must truly reckon with the conditions of our existence. We must reckon with how we are limited, and also with the reality that we are free and therefore responsible for our possibilities. Beauvoir takes such an admission to be a hopeful one, writing, "It is in the knowledge of the genuine conditions of our life that we must draw our strength to live and our reason for acting" (([1947] 1976, 9). For her, the ambiguity of our existence is the very source of our creativity, of our freedom, and our capacity to make and remake the world and ourselves. "The notion of ambiguity," she writes, "must not be confused with that of absurdity. To declare that existence is absurd is to deny that it can ever be given a meaning; to say that it is ambiguous is to assert that its meaning is never fixed, that it must be constantly won" (129).

AN ETHICS OF AMBIGUITY

In "Pyrrhus and Cineas," Beauvoir takes up the questions definitive of her moral period: How can I act in ways that support humanity? What makes an individual or political project ethical or unethical? What is the basis of ethical relationships? In this early work, she begins to develop her existentialist ethics, arguing that each individual must accept responsibility for the fact that their choices and actions produce the conditions within which others act. "Our freedoms support each other like stones in an arch," writes Beauvoir, "but in an arch that no pillars support" ([1944] 2004, 140). She pursues this line of thinking further in *The Ethics of Ambiguity* where she constructs an ethics rooted in our ontological ambiguity most explicitly. A key difference in these two works is that in the latter Beauvoir fully rejects the idea that there is an internal, subjective experience of freedom untouched by others. Rather than insisting on the truth of a radical, ontological freedom, Beauvoir pushes us toward a recognition of moral freedom. She realizes that although we are free, we can also fail to will ourselves and others free. If we are to live ethically, she claims, if we are to be truly free, what matters is how we assume our individual existence in relation to others.

The pursuit of an ethical self-other relation rests on whether we can and do assume our ontological ambiguity. In "Pyrrhus and Cineas" and *The Ethics of Ambiguity*, Beauvoir introduces the concepts of facticity and transcendence to delineate the ambiguous condition of our existence. Beauvoir refers to **facticity** as the givens of being, or that which just is. The factical names, then, the facts that are true in any given circumstance. That there are "things" in the world that I interact with is a fact, whether it is the presence of trees, rocks, light, or even the fact of others' existence. For Beauvoir, a key dimension of facticity is the fact of the body, not as biologically determinative, but in the sense that every subject has a body. There is no escaping this fact of our mortal existence. Insofar as there are inevitable facts at play in our experience, ones I did not choose but just are, facticity is a dimension of constraint in our lives. But, how an individual experiences these facts and what they come to mean is a matter of our transcendent activity. For Beauvoir, **transcendence** is the movement or upsurge of our existence beyond facticity. It is in "Pyrrhus and Cineas" that Beauvoir first begins to develop an account of embodied transcendence. In this work, she describes transcendence as the activity of projection, a movement beyond facticity, through which a subject creates meaning and possibilities for future action. Yet, Beauvoir acknowledges that one's facticity always animates one's possibilities, such that although an individual can transcend facticity, they can never evade it. Our ambiguity lies in the truth that we are never just facticity or transcendence; we are both. What matters is that we *live* both, that we exist in ways wherein one does not obscure the other.

In *The Second Sex*, Beauvoir introduces the notion of **immanence** to indicate the dimension of our existence that is life-sustaining, passive, and cyclical, and thus related to facticity. She continues to describe transcendence as a future-oriented, world-building activity related to the movement of freedom. Here, though, Beauvoir posits immanence and transcendence in more explicit phenomenological terms as two lived dimensions of human existence. She describes our immanence in relation to cyclical time or repetition. In our immanence, she claims, we are existents who experience time and facts happening to us. In contrast, as transcendence, we experience time as ours to make and the world as ours to build and rebuild. In *The Second Sex* and *The Coming of Age*, Beauvoir argues that while all human existence is immanence and transcendence, the particularities of our individual and collective situations, that is how we are socially, historically, economically, and politically situated, will alter whether we are able to assume both modes of our existence.

In these latter works, by drawing attention to how or whether we can live our ambiguity, Beauvoir advances a richer phenomenological account of ambiguity. In these texts, Beauvoir also reveals how a situation of oppression relegates an individual to immanence without possibilities to assume herself as transcendence. For instance, in her investigation of the constraints of patriarchy, Beauvoir argues that women become anchored in, coerced into undertaking, and overwhelmingly expected to sacrifice themselves to life-sustaining, cyclical activities such as reproductive, emotional, and domestic labor. In Beauvoir's view, the result is that women are kept from transcendent activity, which, in patriarchy, is taken to be the domain of men. The outcome is a perversion of human existence, which erodes the condition for realizing moral freedom, insofar as living our ambiguity is a necessary condition for moral freedom. We must, then, Beauvoir posits, undertake projects and self-other relations that affirm ambiguity.

For Beauvoir, to succeed or fail in such activity hinges on how one pursues what she names "the desire to be" and "the desire to disclose being" ([1947] 1976, 8–9). *The Ethics of Ambiguity* opens with an account of intentionality in which Beauvoir describes these two desires. **Intentionality** is a phenomenological concept that describes consciousness as a directedness toward an object; it is to be 'conscious of' an object. Beauvoir understands embodied consciousness as activity that brings the world and meaning into existence. As embodied subjects, we move toward "things" in the world, whether they be objects or other beings. This movement is not fixed by causal rules of nature or a supernatural power; rather, it is the movement of a subject's engagement with their world through which we come into existence as distinct individuals. For Beauvoir, the intentionality of consciousness operates through the two modes of desire. As she explains in *The Ethics of Ambiguity*, the first kind of desire—the desire to be—is a matter of making oneself a lack of being. For one to come into their individuated existence, they must uproot themself, distinguishing themself from that which they are not; doing so makes them present in the world.

To concretize this point, take an example Beauvoir uses. When an individual looks out onto an open landscape, they are "conscious of" what is before them—a blue sky, a grassy field, perhaps the sound of birds. The distance between them and the "things" they intend results from the individual experiencing themselves as a lack of being, i.e., they *are not* these other "things." Through this lack, and in being conscious of the field of "things" in all its distinctness and difference, an individual affirms themselves as a distinct self, or as what Beauvoir calls "a positive existence" ([1947] 1976, 13). In experiencing themselves as a lack of being, an individual gives meaning to their existence. For this reason, "the desire to be" is the activity of desiring the very meaning of one's being. This first desire opens up the second desire of "wanting to disclose being" (12). The activity of disclosure is the articulation of meaning, not of finding meaning in the world, but of bringing meaning into the world. The second kind of desire—the desire to disclose being—is to pursue the openness of one's existence.

As will be explored more thoroughly in the following chapter, Beauvoir gives a moral dimension to these desires, arguing that human activity often gets anchored in the desire to be, working to fix or ground existence in order to temper the anxiety that existence is ultimately indeterminate. This would be the move or intention of turning becoming into being, affirming an essence of existence to resolve the anxiety of indeterminacy. She thus locates ethical success in taking comfort and delight in this second kind of desire, in attending to meaning-making rather than fixing meaning. While our intentional activity is not inherently ethical, the very meaning of existence, the very values that animate existence, and the very possibility for affirming our ambiguity, emerges from the intentional activity of our existence.

In Beauvoir's view, we struggle to engage in intentional activity that avows our ambiguity. She draws our attention to this reality, though abstractly, in *The Ethics of Ambiguity* where she describes six figures that illustrate various modes of existence: the sub-man, the serious man, the nihilist, the adventurer, the passionate man, and the free man. She positions them on a moral ladder, with the sub-man being at the very bottom; he is the subject who refuses his ambiguity to an extreme by annihilating his transcendence. Beauvoir describes the sub-man as feeling only the facticity of his existence. Immersed in being, he relies on static meanings and predetermined, fixed values.

In doing so, he refuses his transcendence ([1947] 1976. 44). For this reason, Beauvoir claims he becomes dangerous. In finding "refuge in the ready-made values" and "shelter behind a label," he is the kind of person who readily takes orders and is willing to do "the actual dirty work" of oppressive movements (44). He is "afraid of engaging himself in a project as he is afraid of being disengaged and thereby being in a state of danger before the future, in the midst of its possibilities" (44). He deals with his existential fear by renouncing his own transcendence and falling in line with fanaticism and tyrannical values that further annihilate his subjectivity but protect him from the indeterminacy of the future (44). He takes shelter in what Beauvoir calls "the serious world" of ready-made values. In refusing his transcendence, and so too relinquishing the desire to disclose being, he disavows his ambiguity and destroys his bond with others. Like the sub-man, the serious man is also a dangerous mode of flight from ambiguity. The serious man dedicates his life to an external goal and pursues it relentlessly regardless of how it impacts others. But, in contrast to the sub-man who refuses his transcendence, the serious man assumes his transcendence in ways that subordinate others. Whereas the sub-man withdraws immediately from his transcendence and finds an external order to obey, the serious man casts himself into the world only to will himself into existence through a violent, fanatical project.

In "An Eye for An Eye" ([1946] 2004), Beauvoir examines the moral fault of a serious man more concretely. Written in the aftermath of witnessing the trial and execution of Robert Brasillach, an author and fascist who conspired with the Nazi regime and revealed the whereabouts of French Jews to aid in their persecution, this essay of Beauvoir's is at once a reflection on the desire and ethics of revenge and an attempt to define what makes Brasillach's acts an absolute evil. Regarding the latter, Beauvoir makes an early reference to her notion of ambiguity to account for absolute evil as a deliberate effort of degradation, by which she means reducing a subject to a thing. On her account, what makes Brasillach's actions unambiguously evil is that he turns himself into a sovereign subject who renders others into pure objects. Pursuing his existence in this way is the condition that enables him to participate in the Nazi project of genocide.

He justifies the violence by turning himself into a supreme subject and turning others into total objects. This justification is thus predicated on the refusal to affirm the ambiguity of existence, namely that he, like the other, is always subject *and* object.

At the top of Beauvoir's moral ladder, is the free man, who she describes as the kind of subject who assumes his transcendence without renouncing the weight of facticity. To do so means he does not pursue freedom only for his own sake. He does not live as if he is unbounded and alone in the world; he does not elevate his existence above that of others, and he desires to disclose meaning, to open the future by taking the risk to live out a project that affirms the projects of others. In contrast to the free man, the sub-man refuses this risk, while the serious man refuses the existence of others. The nihilist, however, refuses transcendence by positing the world and his existence as meaningless. The adventurer and the passionate man are both the kinds of subjects who affirm their transcendence; where they go wrong, however, is that they elevate their projects above others. The adventurer, pursuing leisure and enjoyment, "regards mankind as indifferent matter destined to support the game of his existence" ([1947] 1976, 62). The passionate man, who populates the world with meaning and thus partakes in the desire to disclose being, is too enveloped in his own project. He pursues it without ever finding fulfillment in the world, without ever focusing on his relations with others. Although the adventurer and passionate man realize their existence in ways closer to that of the free man, they still pursue transcendence at the expense of their facticity. Ultimately, what we must strive for is to become the free man.

On her own account, however, *The Ethics of Ambiguity* is dissatisfying. "Of all my books, it is the one that irritates me the most today," Beauvoir writes in the third volume of her autobiography, *Forces of Circumstance* ([1963] 1992a, 67). Central to her irritation is the fact that the moral issues and figures she describes are too abstract, too far removed from the concrete situation that motivated her thinking in the first place. "My descriptions ... the attitudes I examine are explained by objective conditions; I limited myself to isolating their moral significance to such an extent that my portraits are not situated on any level of reality," Beauvoir writes. "I was in error when I thought I could define a morality independent of a social context" (67). She makes a similar critique of several of her political essays, writing, "What I find hard is the idealism that blemishes these essays. In reality, men defined themselves for me by their bodies, their needs, their work; I set no form, no value above the individual of flesh and blood" (68). She laments the abstract route she took to justify material needs: "Why did I write *concrete liberty* instead of *bread*, and subordinate the will to live with a search for the meaning of life? I never brought matters down to saying: People must eat because they are hungry" (68).

Where her philosophical work may fall short in this respect, her novels do not. For instance, Beauvoir's second novel, *The Blood of Others*, offers a more concrete illustration of what it means to engage in ethical activity. Published in 1945, two years before *The Ethics of Ambiguity*, *The Blood of Others* takes place in Nazi-occupied Paris where the main characters Hélène and Jean are both faced with distinct decisions about how to act and who to become. Jean, the leader of a resistance group, is initially bonded to others and actively pursues his responsibility to secure that bond. But when Jean's friend is killed in a political demonstration, he retreats and refuses involvement with the resistance. This choice to disengage leads Jean into passive complicity with the occupation. His passivity, Beauvoir shows us, is a flight from transcendence. Hélène, in contrast, is not initially engaged in resistance. She temporarily flees the occupation for safety, but in doing so, she comes to witness and become conscious of the suffering of the Jewish people. This concrete encounter, actualized through her own spontaneous movement, leads her to join the resistance. Eventually, she is shot and killed in a resistance activity; her passive complicity turns into sacrificial political action. It is important that Hélène's moral conversion actualizes in relation to events in which she experiences herself as an object for others, namely when she is gazed upon by those who are suffering. The gaze of others leads Hélène to realize she is not a pure subject, that she is not alone in the world and unattached to others.

Whereas Jean flees his transcendence and disavows his ambiguity, Hélène comes to reckon with her ambiguity and pursues ethical action. In showing this difference between Jean and Hélène, Beauvoir is not advancing a moral thesis about the particularities of how to act in a specific encounter. Instead, as she explains in *Force of Circumstance*, the point is to reveal the paradox of a subject's experience of freedom and the infringement on one's freedom by others. What we do with that infringement, whether we assume our ambiguity or refuse it, is paramount to Beauvoir's conception of ethical action.

To further clarify Beauvoir's ethics, we can look to her third novel, *All Men are Mortal* ([1946] 1955), which offers a critique of ethics removed from ambiguity. In this novel, Beauvoir depicts the life of a man and political leader, Fosca, who becomes immortal. In various centuries, he aspires to lead his people to happiness and prosperity, but in evading his finitude, his perspective becomes far removed from the concrete realities of mortal existence. Even when acting benevolently, Fosca pursues universal values, ones that are ahistorical and abstracted from the specific problems of a given time. What we learn through Fosca's immortality is that his pursuit of the universal is bound up with his immortality; he cannot grasp the significance of engaging the concrete because he has removed himself from it. In exiling himself from the concrete by embracing immortality, Fosca loses his relation to moral freedom for, on Beauvoir's account, it is found only by pursuing a finite and bounded existence. "Lacking mortality he is left with nothing personal to hope for," write Beauvoir scholars Edward and Kate Fullbrook. "He belongs to no age and to no place; his life is boundless and therefore without shape, without risk, without meaning, without value" (1998, 50). When Fosca flees his mortality, he renounces his immanence, and as immortal his transcendent activity is uninvolved and unresponsive to concrete, historical circumstances. This is a dangerous position to occupy. In sacrificing his finitude and denying his immanence, Fosca spends his life waging and witnessing war and destruction.

In contrast to the pursuit of morality through the immortal and abstract, Beauvoir's existentialist ethics offers us a way into the world. We must not evade the concrete and finite. We must not find respite in the abstract and infinite. Accordingly, her existentialist ethics offers us a way into the complex, messy truths of our situation. To be free, we cannot evade our reality like Fosca; we must struggle in the world we are in. As she writes at the end of *The Ethics of Ambiguity*, "existentialism proposes no evasion. On the contrary, its ethics is experienced in the truth of life ... If it came to be that each man did what he must, existence would be saved in each one without there being any need of dreaming of a paradise where all would be reconciled in death" ([1947] 1976, 159).

In insisting that we each do what we must, Beauvoir underscores the individualism of her ethics. Yet, "[t]his individualism," she writes in the conclusion of *The Ethics of Ambiguity*, "does not lead toward the anarchy of the personal whim" (156). Rather, her turn to the individual underscores that it is of paramount importance to making meaning and values that forge our bond with others. For this reason, her existentialist ethics is neither egoistic nor solipsistic. In her view, to act only for our own self-interest would amount to an existential isolationism, a position that relies on a perception of oneself as sovereign and unbounded. Her ethics is also not a form of relativism. Although she rejects moral absolutes, she roots all ethical action in freedom. We must always, she argues, pursue our concrete, finite lives in ways that simultaneously affirm our individual freedom and the freedom of others. Ultimately, in the face of any form of evil or oppression, Beauvoir puts the responsibility on each of us, to act in ways that affirm the ambiguity of the human condition and treat freedom as a situated, lived phenomenon.

SITUATED FREEDOM

When Beauvoir talks about the pursuit of freedom, she is not advancing a universal account of free will. She is not interested in freedom in the abstract. She is advancing a deeply political and concrete account of freedom. What is unique and significant about Beauvoir's conception of freedom, then, is that she conceives of freedom as a situated phenomenon. In her view, our understanding of freedom must not be abstracted or universalized from the conditions in which we *live* freedom. She takes seriously that social and political dimensions of existence can distort and work to render impossible a lived relation to freedom and she works to articulate how and when such foreclosure occurs. In an interview with German feminist Alice Schwarzer, Beauvoir puts it this way: "I insisted on the fact that there are situations where freedom cannot be exercised, or where it is simply a mystification" (1984, 109).

Of her philosophical works, it is first in "Pyrrhus and Cineas" that Beauvoir works to develop an account of situated freedom, drawing attention to the way others impinge on our freedom. "I am," she writes, "the face of the other's misery ... I am the facticity of their situation" ([1944] 2004, 126). Insofar as the intersubjective condition of existence is an inescapable fact, an individual always has the power to affect the other's freedom. This reality means that freedom is not a given, but achieved and exercised through how we relate to one another. Kristana Arp traces a distinction between power and freedom in *The Ethics of Ambiguity*, starting with Beauvoir's assertion that "the freedom of man is infinite, but his power is limited" (Arp 2001, 28). Arp accounts for the distinction between freedom and power as the difference between ontological freedom and the social, material, and political conditions of moral freedom, highlighting that Beauvoir's conception of moral freedom is shaped by the concrete conditions in which we can assume it. Arp aptly notes that Beauvoir does not explicitly tease out the relationship between power and freedom. Nevertheless, Beauvoir is adamant that our engagement with the concreteness of the world gives freedom its content such that our lived experience of freedom, and the development of our moral freedom, is always limited by material conditions. Those material conditions, the ones formative to our situation, are the basis for our experience of freedom. Far from an abstract understanding of power, then, Beauvoir takes power to be a phenomenon generated in and generative of the concrete conditions of the world. It is not just that an individual has power by virtue of existing, but rather one's power—its shape, its limits, or lack thereof, its content—is a consequence of a subject's lived experience within a given social, political, economic, and historical scene. The power one has is, therefore, a contingent feature of our experience of freedom. So, while all human beings may have the capacity for freedom, whether we experience or live it is conditioned by how we join with others and how other people limit us. While Beauvoir gestures to this situated and phenomenologically grounded conception of freedom as early as "Pyrrhus and Cineas" and further advanced it in *The Ethics of Ambiguity*, it is not until she authors her feminist account of freedom in *The Second Sex* that this claim is most concretely and thoroughly developed.

However, Beauvoir's earlier fiction works are clear precursors to the account of freedom found in *The Second Sex*. In her only play, *Useless Mouths* ([1945] 2011), Beauvoir examines how, in the fictional city-state of Vaucelles, a medieval village in Belgium, women are rendered "useless mouths" by men, and become disposable. In the play, Vaucelles is under siege and food supplies are diminished. To maintain the strength of its army of men, it is decided that women and children, as well as the old and infirm, will be exiled, pushed out of the village and into the hands of the enemy. The justification of this decision rests on a decision about utility. The women, for instance, are rendered useless through a minimization of the value of their labor. This is not an objective valuation of women, however. Beauvoir is clear that their devaluation is rooted in the relations of power central to Vaucelles. The men of Vaucelles, individually and collectively, seize their power by asserting themselves as having the right to delineate who is useful and who is useless. In doing so, they capitalize on their material conditions in a way that destroys the social bond necessary for moral freedom. The moral fault of men is that they do not define themselves in relation to the other, in this case, women. Instead, they define the world through and for themselves only. As a result, women's power is diminished by the material conditions of their situation to the extent that they are reduced to things that can be discarded. Far from being an abstract thought experiment, *Useless Mouths* is a direct commentary on tyrannous, fascist, patriarchal, and capitalist economic and social arrangements in which some individuals are deemed useless and thus "other," making them not only existentially worthless but materially disposable. *Useless Mouths* makes clear the horrors that come from concrete conditions in which individuals do not limit their own power and wield it to limit the power of others.

That which shapes one's relation to freedom is not simply external, however. Certainly, the social, political, and economic conditions of one's existence are deeply significant, but Beauvoir's phenomenological orientation reminds us that freedom is an embodied phenomenon. Especially in *The Second Sex* and *The Coming of Age*, she draws attention to how the lived body is mediated by dominant values and norms to such an extent that our bodily experiences and processes disclose realities of domination, as well as those of privilege and oppression. In *The Second Sex*, for instance, Beauvoir shows how a woman lives an impoverished relation to freedom in large part because of how she experiences her body-self in the world. A woman comes to experience her body and so, too, her whole self as violable, as intensely infringed upon by others, as an object, as weak and fragile, as that which should be adorned, among a host of other conflicting and contradictory messages that structure and give shape to a woman's bodily comportment because of the power and persistence of patriarchal values and norms. It is not, then, only that power shuts down freedom from the outside. Rather, power gets "inside" and comes to actualize particular modes of embodiment.

Central to this phenomenological consideration of how freedom is lived in situation, or whether freedom can be lived at all, is an account of the temporal contours of situated experience. In contrast to clock time and historical time, phenomenologists account for temporality as the subjective experience of time. For Beauvoir, our individual existence is temporally structured, developmentally and existentially, by the past, present, and future. But unlike classical phenomenological accounts of time that insist on a general experience of time, namely that we all experience a flow of the past, present, and future, Beauvoir understands temporality to be entangled with social and historical conditions and meanings. For her, our lived experience of time discloses our relation to freedom. As Beauvoir sees it, for a subject to assume herself as a freedom, she must live a concrete relation to *her* future as indeterminate and open. In *The Ethics of Ambiguity*, Beauvoir describes an impoverished relation to the future as having a ceiling over one's head, which deeply restricts one's future horizon. Instead of expansion, there is closure. In *The Second Sex*, Beauvoir focuses on how a subject's past and present are mediated by others, as well as by the values of the world in which one lives. In doing so, she exposes how an open and dynamic relation to time, an experience in which the future is opened by the past and present, is not lived by women because the material conditions of their lives do not grant it. This feminist insight exposes how a triadic structure of time, an experience of a flowing past, present, and future, is not a given of human existence but is instead conferred by the material conditions in which one lives. In effect, how we live time is, for Beauvoir, indicative of whether or not we are free.

On Beauvoir's account, then, freedom is not a mere idea nor is it solely a formal arrangement codified by law. Freedom is embodied and lived out in very visceral, material ways. For her, freedom is not an autonomous experience, but a relational event; it is a movement toward an open future dependent on and tethered to how one is perceived, valued, and treated by others. Consequently, freedom cannot be realized through abstract moral and political commitments. Beauvoir's situated freedom requires a reckoning with the concrete, tangible, social, and material world right in front of us. It requires affirming our bond with others intimately, socially, and politically.

RESPONSIBILITY: RISK, CONFLICT, AND APPEAL

To meet the conditions of the ethical, Beauvoir claims, an individual's lived freedom must embrace the ties that bind them to others. That is, freedom must affirm the self-other relation, rather than obscure or destroy it. For Beauvoir, then, genuine freedom is not a self-interested reality. "[I]t is not true that the recognition of the freedom of others limits my own freedom: to be free is not to have the power to do anything you like," she asserts in *The Ethics of Ambiguity* ([1947] 1976, 91). "[I]t is to be able to surpass the given toward an open future; the existence of others as a freedom defines my situation and is even the condition of my own freedom. I am oppressed if I am thrown into prison, but not if I am kept from throwing my neighbor into prison" (91). Accordingly, freedom is a matter of becoming responsible for how we engage with others.

To engage ethically means each subject must limit their own power and pursue their individual life in ways that take care of the other, in ways that are generative of the self-other bond. To do so, however, is not an easy task. The pursuit of moral freedom is laden with risk and conflict, and it rests on creating conditions in which we can live in solidarity with one another, a point discussed in detail Chapter 6.

For Beauvoir, **risk** is the inescapable uncertainty that lies at the heart of every project; it is the reality that there is no guarantee that others will affirm any project I undertake or that my project will have the outcomes I desire. In fact, to become a particular individual in the world, to intend the world, consciously and unconsciously, in the way that makes you who you are, is to engage and embody risk. Risk is a matter of how others will respond to your project. Will others endorse my project? Will they alter it? Will they reject it? What will happen to me in the face of these responses? These weighty questions, often generative of existential angst, are present for each subject because of the fact of the other's existence. Since I am not alone in the world, my project can only be sustained if others take it up. My project is contingent on their response. We need others to engage in our projects and there is no guarantee they will. In fact, the reality is that their projects may conflict with mine. The existential risk of my project is rooted in both the general fact that it is mine and not the other's project, and it is also rooted in the content of my project. What is at stake in the values my project advances and the meanings it creates? Does my project affirm the status quo, or does it challenge it? Does my project refuse violence or does it sustain it? Ultimately, the intensity of the risk of my project and indeed the conflict that may emerge from it has much to do with what kind of world my project seeks to create or affirm.

In "Pyrrhus and Cineas," Beauvoir claims there is inevitable conflict at the heart of freedom. The conflict is not that the self is doomed to struggle against others. Rather, the conflict is a result of the finite and singular character of our existence, namely that we are mortal, situated, and individuated. In establishing myself as a particular subject through my projects, I separate myself from others. This separation is a positing of a "me," an emergence of my singularity through which I become distinguishable from the other. Such separation need not negate others in the sense that my separation from them seeks their degradation or annihilation, although it could, and, historically, many projects have. But, for Beauvoir, the separation that results from this singularity nonetheless makes intersubjective conflict inevitable. As distinctly situated individuals we will not share the same project, and this, she claims, positions the other as an obstacle to my project. First, an individual must determine how to engage others in their difference. And, individuals may pursue conflicting values, which means there is always the danger that others may undertake projects that do not affirm my own project. Or, as she puts it in *The Ethics of Ambiguity*, "it is evident that we are not going to decide to fulfill the will of every man. There are cases where a man positively wants evil, that is, the enslavement of other men, and he must then be fought" ([1947] 1976, 136).

In instances of social or political evil, Beauvoir does not advocate compromise. Some values must be rejected. For example, finding a middle ground when it comes to ending a particular historical legacy of oppression and violence may be possible, but not ethical. That she rules compromise out does not mean we cannot or should not work to reconcile conflict. We should take the risk to pursue dialogue, but we also might need to fight against the projects of others. In the face of conflict, Beauvoir also does not rule out violence as a response. In fact, she argues that it *may* be a necessary means to secure freedom, but it must be justified concretely. When or if there should be recourse to violence relies on whether it opens concrete possibilities to freedom. Importantly, our intimate relations are not ruled out of such conflict, a point she shows time and time again in her novels. Love is an experience that draws the other into proximity and thus is ripe with the possibility of conflict. It is also an experience that can be rooted, overtly and tacitly, in values and patterns of domination. Such relations must also be rejected.

At the same time, we are not doomed to conflict and violence because, Beauvoir insists, we have the capacity to take responsibility for our actions. Indeed, as was discussed previously, our moral freedom relies on the pursuit of a project that wills the self and other free. We can, then, diminish the chance for conflict by making sure our actions do not compromise the freedom of others. To do so is not, however, a simple task. Beauvoir does not claim moral freedom to be easy to come by, but she does insist it is worth pursuing repeatedly. It is this point that makes her existentialist ethics one of hope, rather than one of despair. Our aim should be to repeat projects that secure moral freedom.

Her account of the pursuit of moral freedom in the face of inevitable conflict relies on another important notion, that of the appeal. Whereas risk is the uncertainty of how my project will unfold in relation to others, namely whether it will be altered, rejected, or denied, the appeal of my project is the activity of calling on others to take it up and affirm it, including the values that underpin it. On Beauvoir's account, the appeal is that which moves us toward others, beyond our singularity. As philosopher Debra Bergoffen (1997) writes, "The appeal is the condition of the possibility of a human community. In responding to my appeal you demonstrate that there is no pre-given human bond, 'we' relationships are possible" (51). So, whereas the ontology of transcendence positions the other as an obstacle and conflictual existence, the appeal is what opens us to each other. As Beauvoir develops the notion of the appeal in her early works, she underscores that an ethical appeal is that which is the condition for a bond between self and other; it forms a "we."

When in an ethical mode, an appeal must be made to the other in their freedom. I cannot force my project on others. Other people must be free to reject my appeal, which is where we find the risk of and potential conflict in any project. However, given the limits of situation, it is not always the case that an ethical appeal is possible. Some situations prohibit the possibility of rejection. Contexts that are overtly or subtly coercive, that are manipulative, or that demand compliance, are the kinds of conditions that undermine the possibility for rejecting an appeal, and thus that also undermine the realization of moral freedom. We must, then, strive for political and material conditions that make the ethical appeal possible. If there are conditions that prohibit or silence me from sharing my project with others, then, as a condition of my own freedom, I must struggle against them. If there are others who are unable to respond to me, I must work to create a world in which they can engage me. Those who are struggling to survive, those who are mired in meeting their basic needs, those who are incarcerated, anyone who is not materially able to respond to me and engage me as a peer in the sense that they are also free to make and reject appeals, I must work to create material and political conditions that allow them to become peers. That is, I must struggle against their oppression and subordination in order for ethical appeals to be possible.

Many appeals do not meet the criteria of Beauvoir's ethics. Appeals can be superficial. Appeals can be made that negate the other's existence, whether unknowingly or intentionally. Appeals can be made only to secure my values at the expense of the other. Indeed, Beauvoir's work shows that appeals can be dangerous, as in the case of Hitler, and pernicious, as in the case of patriarchy, and they can also be a flight from ethics, as in the case of the Marquis de Sade, who she writes about in her essay "Must We Burn Sade?" ([1951–52] 2012). However, an appeal can also be a commitment to justice and our bonds with others, as was the case with Beauvoir in her anti-colonial dissent against the French government and political support of Djamila Boupacha, which is discussed further in Chapter 7. Although we are separated and individual, we must strive to create projects and values that bring us together, that form an ethical bond between self-other. Such an undertaking, as is discussed in Chapter 6, is to realize solidarity, a political phenomenon that Beauvoir takes to be a necessary condition of ethical existence.

Such ethical striving is preempted by what, in *The Ethics of Ambiguity* Beauvoir calls "the serious world" ([1947] 1976, 35). The serious world is a particular kind of moral world wherein ready-made values, static labels, and unambiguous moral categories orient one in the world and circumscribe the projects one undertakes. In childhood, she claims, the serious world is a part of moral development, intended to shelter children from the adult world, to allow them to live in innocence, without the anguish of freedom and the heavy burden of responsibility. The trouble with the serious world, however, is that it operates in ways that compromise a child's relation to transcendence. Children only learn to become, to cultivate projects, within a universe that has been set up for them.

In the serious world, adults dictate how the world is and who children will become, thus reifying values and meanings that may need to be abandoned. However, she also describes the serious world as more than a phase of moral development, contrasting it to what she calls the infantile world. Such a world is the world of those who are kept in a state of servitude and ignorance—the concrete examples she uses are the situations of slaves and women, whom she describes being situated in the world as "grown up children." In each of these situations, the infantile world "is stretched over their heads," and "they can exercise their freedom, but only within the universe which has been set up for them" (37). The serious world, propped up as morally superior and inhabited by those with power, towers over those situated in the infantile world.

In its various concrete manifestations, what the serious world does is teach the moral values, meanings, and dispositions of the dominant world; it places a ceiling over who we can and will become. In doing so, we embody the serious world not necessarily because we consciously take it up but because it structures our existence. The ethical problem with the serious world is that, in insisting that values and meanings are predetermined and static, it compromises our ability to affirm our ambiguity, which preempts the possibilities we have for assuming responsibility for our actions and realizing ethical projects, and therefore compromises our capacity to make an ethical appeal.

Given the conditions of her world, and that of ours, there is a lot that stands in the way, that forestalls or forecloses, the prohibits even the possibility for an experience of freedom that meets Beauvoir's conditions of the ethical. But such a reality does not mean we should not undertake the risk and appeal of the ethical. Indeed, for her, we must. Whatever situations of harm, violence, or oppression we are faced with, whether they are interpersonal, social, economic, or political, it is on us to change it. And we can, so long as we are willing to assume responsibility for our freedom and that of others. This is where the hope for humanity lies. Whether we succeed or fail depends, Beauvoir argues, on whether we assume our existence in bad faith or in authenticity. It is this point that will be the topic of the next chapter.

SUGGESTED READING

Primary Texts

Beauvoir, Simone de. [1944] 2004. "Pyrrhus and Cineas." In *Simone de Beauvoir: Philosophical Writings*, translated by Marybeth Timmerman, edited by Margaret Simons, 89–149. Urbana: University of Illinois Press.

———— [1945] 1964. *The Blood of Others*. Translated by Yvonne Moyse and Roger Senhouse. New York: Penguin Books.

———— [1945] 2011. "The Useless Mouths." In *Simone de Beauvoir: "The Useless Mouths" and Other Literary Writings*, translated by Liz Stanley and Catherine Naji, edited by Margaret Simons and Marybeth Timmerman, 9–89. Urbana: University of Illinois Press.

———— [1946] 1955. *All Men Are Mortal*. Translated by Leonard M. Friedman. Cleveland: World Publishing.

———— [1946] 2004, "An Eye for an Eye." In *Simone de Beauvoir: Philosophical Writings*, translated by Kristana Arp, edited by Margaret Simons, 245–260. Urbana: University of Illinois Press.

———— [1947] 1976. *The Ethics of Ambiguity*. Translated by Bernard Frechtman. New York: Citadel Press.

———— 1947 [2004]. "What is Existentialism?" In *Simone de Beauvoir: Philosophical Writings*, translated by Marybeth Timmerman, edited by Margaret Simons, 323–326. Urbana: University of Illinois Press.

Secondary Texts

Arp, Kristana. 2001. *The Bonds of Freedom: Simone de Beauvoir's Existentialist Ethics*. Chicago: Open Court.

Bergoffen, Debra. 1997. *The Philosophy of Simone de Beauvoir: Gendered Phenomenologies, Erotic Generosities*. Albany, NY: State University of New York Press.

Fullbrook, Edward and Kate Fullbrook. 1998. *Simone de Beauvoir: A Critical Introduction*. Cambridge: Polity Press.

Kruks, Sonia. 1990. *Situation and Human Existence: Freedom, Subjectivity and Society*, New York: Routledge.

————. 2012. *Simone de Beauvoir and the Politics of Ambiguity*, Oxford: Oxford University Press.

3

HOW SHOULD I LIVE?

In her prestigious Goncourt prize novel, *The Mandarins*, published in 1954, Beauvoir tells the story of a group of Parisian
intellectuals who, in the immediate aftermath of French liberation in 1944, struggle to place themselves in the new post-war
world. The story centers on fallout among the group. In the
absence of their previous resistance activity against the Vichy
regime, the intellectuals no longer have a common purpose
uniting them. They are drawn into dilemmas and conflict about
what actions to choose for themselves and for others, a matter
that is more perplexing for each of them in peacetime. During
the war, resisting evil was their clear purpose. But, in the years
after the war, they are each once again burdened with the question of how to live. As *The Mandarins* makes evident, it is up to
each of us to choose what to live for. For Beauvoir, the question
is a deeply individual one not because her ethics are characterized by individualism. Rather, the question begins with the
subject because it is the individual who chooses what actions to
undertake. It is because of this reality of choice that Beauvoir
was acutely preoccupied with the question: How should I live?

In the absence of a pre-given nature, human existence
requires ethics; we need to create and establish what it means
to be good or to do evil, and what it means to treat others well.
From Beauvoir's perspective, when we, as individuals, refuse
this condition of our existence, we run from our freedom. Our
freedom, then, is always entangled with the ethical, even if we
don't realize it. As Jean, one of the main characters in her novel
The Blood of Others, reminds us, "I think that where you go

DOI: 10.4324/9781003399995-3

wrong is that you imagine that your reasons for living ought to fall on you, ready-made from heaven, whereas we have to find them in ourselves" ([1945] 1964, 71).

Beauvoir was no stranger to the complexity of living an ethical life. Across her work she explores the external and internal obstacles that preempt us from and even encourage us to flee moral freedom. But she is also adamant that each of us can and must strive to live ethically in the world with others. She is insistent that we must not assume a life where anything goes or allow for a world where a "to each their own" ideology prevails. As discussed in Chapter 2, Beauvoir's conception of freedom entails a profound responsibility to others, to the mutual recognition and respect of the freedom of both self and other. What, then, does it look like for each subject to pursue and assume a bond with others?

Beauvoir's answer can be found in her concept of **authenticity** and its counter **bad faith**. In *Being and Nothingness* ([1943] 2018), Sartre describes bad faith (*mauvaise fois*) as a mode of existence in which a subject reduces themselves or others to a static existence. This, he claims, is a kind of self-deception in which a subject takes themself or others to be that which they are not. For instance, I could treat an individual as a mere object, as *only* a vehicle through which I get my desires met, and thereby refuse their subject status. For Sartre, bad faith functions as a moral vice and all of us are equally lured into it by the demands of society. For Beauvoir, bad faith is also a moral fault. She similarly describes it as a way of assuming one's situated existence that denies ambiguity and, as a result, is a flight from moral freedom. Beauvoir, however, does not think we are all equally lured into bad faith. In her view, whether we live in bad faith has much to do with what the material and political conditions of our lives offer us. It is often the case, Beauvoir insists, that how the world is set up, and how our lives are structured by its arrangements can entice us to assume bad faith, and even preempt a self-awareness that one is in bad faith. This is the point she develops in *The Second Sex* when she considers how patriarchal values lure us into bad faith. But Beauvoir doesn't shy away from suggesting that even if we are set up to live in bad faith, there is still an ethical choice to make in the face of the world, even when we are deeply constrained by it. The work may be hard to do, but we can, and should, undertake it. We should pursue living authentically. This pursuit is not a matter of becoming fully transparent to oneself or coming to complete and total knowledge of one's aims and intentions. As situated, ambiguous, and free beings, we are never fully present to ourselves and always in process, which means total self-possession is not possible. What Beauvoir has in mind is a kind of authenticity that allows us to relate to others in ways that realize moral freedom.

As this chapter explores, Beauvoir's account of authenticity stands out in several respects. In the mainstream, authenticity is often packaged as "being true to yourself." This kind of authenticity relies on a view that the self can be transparent to itself, and that the self assumes a state from which "I know who I am." In contrast, Beauvoir's understanding of authenticity is a matter of an endless striving to pursue our individuality knowing that oneself is never complete, never an enclosed whole. There is no inner truth to discover, only the ceaseless creation of meaning and values. For Beauvoir, an individual's pursuit of authenticity isn't just for themself. It is a particular mode of being in relation with others. In this sense, authenticity is and is not an individual activity; it is mine to do and therefore it is an autonomous activity, but I do not undertake it only for my sake. Further, contrary to views that posit authenticity as a quest for happiness, Beauvoir's authenticity is a quest for freedom. It is not about individual satisfaction or gratification, but responsibility. Beauvoirian authenticity is, then, a particular way of relating to ourselves, others, and the world through which we realize freedom.

It is because authenticity is the concept through which Beauvoir delineates an ethical mode of existence that it is worthy of focused consideration. She describes and illustrates what it means to embody authenticity across her novels and philosophical works. Given that her descriptions of authenticity appear in relation to her notion of bad faith, understanding the latter is key to reckoning with how to live an authentic life. Both modes of existence are a matter of the choices we make in the world, of how we choose our projects, and of how we choose to exist in relation to others.

CHOICE AND SELF-WILLING

Whether or not one assumes an authentic existence has everything to do with the choices they make. Yet, for Beauvoir, choice is not a simple matter. In contrast to liberal conceptions that take choice to be a matter of autonomous self-willing, of choosing to pull oneself up out of the mess and muck of the world to achieve a better existence for oneself, Beauvoir takes **existential choice** to be a constrained affair. It is not the case, she insists, that we can choose to do whatever we want or even become whoever we want. As situated and ambiguous, our existence is not purely or entirely up to us. What we choose, what we can choose, and the ease with which we are able to choose from an open array of possibilities, is conditioned by values, norms, meanings, and social and economic arrangements that mediate and structure our lived experience. In other words, individual choice is deeply impacted and shaped by others and the world in which we live. What we choose is shaped and inflected by our circumstances, even if we refuse to recognize this to be the case. As will soon be discussed, Beauvoir understands such refusal to be in bad faith.

A central feature of circumstance that mediates and constrains choice is the reality that we always exist in the world with others. Insofar as we are never alone in the world, others always touch our existence and we theirs. What we can choose is conditioned by this reality. Others open and close possibilities for an individual. In her novels, Beauvoir often explores this reality through the experience of intimacy, a condition that allows subjects to closely impact one another's choices. In *The Blood of Others*, Jean laments this reality as he watches his love, Hélène, suffer:

> what kind of choice had I given her? Could she choose that I love her? That I should not exist? That she should not have met me? To leave her free was still tantamount to deciding for her; to remain inactive and docile to her will, was still to create by my own authority a situation to which she could not submit.
>
> ([1945] 1964, 130)

For Jean, as is often the case in love, being in close relation to the other can radically alter how we structure their capacity to choose, both in terms of what they choose and with regard to the affective dimension of choice. A second way Beauvoir considers the mediation and constraint of individual choice has to do with the fact that we are thrown into a world we did not choose. That is, the historical background of our lives plays a role in what choices we can make. This historicity of choice means the content of choice is framed for us by the circumstances we inherit.

While these first two aspects of constraint are factical, a matter of what it is to exist with others and in the world, Beauvoir also offers a politicized account of how choice is constrained. As Chapter 4 discusses in further detail, in her works that describe concrete conditions of oppression, which include *America Day by Day*, *The Second Sex*, and *The Coming of Age*, she speaks about choice as negatively limited, foreclosed even, by others. For instance, in her description of anti-Black racism in the United States in *America Day by Day*, Beauvoir describes the constraints imposed on Black individuals. "The tragic thing about the situation of blacks in the South," she writes, "is that nothing, absolutely nothing is guaranteed to them" ([1947] 1999, 246). Beauvoir notes that this absence of guarantee undermines the existence of all Black individuals: "In discrimination, whites find both material advantages and the surest means of preventing the black person from raising himself to a status that would allow him to make his claims heard" (247). What Beauvoir understood was that others can create conditions that strip certain subjects of capacious conditions of choice. In this sense, choice is not inherently a privileged phenomenon, but the sociohistorical conditions in which one chooses often make it so.

She also understood a capacious experience of choice to be a gendered phenomenon. In Volume II of *The Second Sex*, she describes how, in patriarchal contexts, girls are raised to become the kinds of subjects who have limited choice. For the girl, Beauvoir insists, there is already a plot hatched for her, one in which she is encouraged and expected to take up and make her own. Central to that socially fabricated plot is that a woman is convinced, during her girlhood and adolescence, to become a vassal for men and their projects, rather than a transcendence in her own right. The consequence is that while, as she becomes a woman, she is still choosing her existence, the structure and content of her choice is so heavily mediated by others that who she can become, and the kind of existence she can choose, is heavily delineated for her by others.

Beauvoir does not take such constraints to be totalizing. An individual is not determined by the constraints on her capacity to choose, even if they bear down on one's existence. As she narrates in *Memoirs of a Dutiful Daughter*, the first volume of her autobiography, Beauvoir's own life was subject to the pressures of her social destiny as a woman, namely that she would marry and have children and then become "overburdened with a thousand tiresome tasks" (([1958] 1959, 60). She managed to cultivate a resistant attitude. "Whenever I thought of my own future," she writes, "this servitude seemed to me so burdensome that I decided I wouldn't have any children; the important thing for me was to be able to form minds and mold characters; I shall be a teacher, I thought" (60). That she could imagine a life for herself beyond marriage and motherhood was not, however, merely a matter of her own self-willing. Beauvoir's parents were invested in her education and her father took delight in her intellectual acuity. As a result, her childhood world was not solely a matter of her learning to accept her social destiny as a wife and mother, which was, at the time, the expected trajectory for a young girl of Beauvoir's social, economic, racial, and religious status. At the same time, when the family's class status declined and her father no longer had a dowry for Beauvoir or her sister Hélène, there was no choice for her parents but to allow their daughters to pursue financial independence. They may not have approved of Beauvoir's choice to pursue philosophy, but that she could make this choice was not something she manifested on her own. This is not to say that Beauvoir had no role to play in her life choices. She clearly had unique desires and responses to her situation, and throughout in her life she undertook efforts to escape the conventions of her milieu. But who she became, and what choices she had, and how she could exercise choice, was never purely up to her either. The combination of the intervention of others, including her parents and teachers, the concrete circumstances of her existence which she did not authorize but was nonetheless subject to, and her individual pursuit of her interests and desires, are central to her lived experience of choice.

To will oneself into a particular kind of life is always, then, a mediated and constrained affair.

Insofar as choice characterizes human existence, Beauvoir refuses to submit our lives to any kind of fate. As free, as capable of choice, we live with its existential burden. Each human has the capacity to become, to make meaning, to choose how to act in the world. Situations can thus be transformed. We can make choices that allow us to become who we are not yet. At the same time, we cannot be certain about what the outcomes of our choices will be. There is no crystal ball. The reality of existential choice, Beauvoir posits, is that it is laden with responsibility. In Beauvoir's view, this moral burden of choice often makes people flee the very conditions of freedom. She thinks we are more likely to yield to the ontological and social constraints of human existence or seek to master them through a false belief in absolute freedom. Both are modes of bad faith, a point that will be returned to shortly. To succeed or fail in assuming in choice hinges on how one pursues the desire to be and the desire to disclose being. As mentioned in Chapter 2, *the desire to be* aims to fix or ground one's existence in order to temper the anxiety that existence is ultimately indeterminate. This would be the move or intention of converting becoming into being. Such a conversion would ascribe an essence to existence as a way to resolve the anxiety of life's indeterminacy. The desire to disclose being is to pursue the openness of existence, to attend to rather than seek to overcome the complexity and plurality of one's situation. Beauvoir locates the ethical success of choice in taking comfort and delight in this second kind of desire.

There is often, however, a conflict between experiencing delight in the desire to disclose being and an individual's will. From an existentialist perspective, one's will is bound to their pursuit of projects, such that to will a project, to bring it into the world, is a matter of making oneself the author of that which is mine, a constitutive act of my present self and the future self I aspire to become. To author a project is thus to avow a self-identity and to pursue one's situation as such. This self-making is significant on Beauvoir's account, but she has her concerns. The will of the project, as the existential attitude of the desire to be, is ethically fraught when it is a mere assertion of autonomy and control of the self. The will of the project must remain modified by delight in the openness of being. As philosopher Debra Bergoffen puts it, an individual must "acknowledge the bond of the 'we' and commit myself to protect it" (1997, 96).

On this view, an authentic choice is not one an individual merely chooses to make their own world since this kind of self-authoring would anchor existence into the will of the project and the desire to be. Nor is an authentic choice one that tethers itself to immanence, for this would refuse the activity of the desire to disclose being altogether.

Authentic choice is one in which a subject takes full responsibility for their choice and the concreteness of circumstance in which a choice is made. As will be discussed shortly, Beauvoir understands authenticity to require these conditions. She also insists that for authenticity to meet the criteria of the ethical, it must not neglect the reality of the other. It is, then, ultimately insufficient to only take responsibility for one's choices. In the end, to be authentic means to engage and pursue freedom with others, and this engagement requires an openness to the ambiguity and indeterminacy of human existence, even as it requires one to self-author and make choices. To assume or take up an authentic existence, one must undertake choice in a way that embraces ambiguity and bears the burden of the ethical demands that follow.

BEING IN BAD FAITH

Bad faith (*la mauvaise foi*) is first and foremost a matter of self-deception or concealment. To be in bad faith refers to a wide range of **existential attitudes**, or a disposition or way of assuming one's existence in the world, which rely on a kind of existence that allows a subject to disavow ambiguity and in doing so, distance oneself from the reality of the human condition. In bad faith, a subject comes to live their life through an illusion of reality. For this reason, bad faith is a matter of lying to oneself about the conditions of existence. Although Beauvoir does not think bad faith always amounts to an ethical problem, what concerns her most is when it does. Central to her preoccupation with bad faith is the way it generates and structures unethical social, material, and political conditions. An individual's illusory engagement with reality has, for Beauvoir, destructive effects on the relationship between self and others and, in her view, is a condition from which freedom can be and is often denied.

As Edward and Kate Fullbrook (1998) point out, Beauvoir characterizes bad faith in two ways: the bad faith of transcendence and the bad faith of immanence. In *She Came to Stay*, she offers an initial characterization of these two modes of bad faith. The novel tells the story of the ambiguously triangulated lives of Pierre, Xavière, and Françoise, the three of whom become entangled in a polyamorous relationship. Set in late 1930s Paris, Pierre and Françoise are in a stable, but open relationship, each free to pursue sexual relationships with others. Highlighting how dynamics of desire and intimacy intensify the encounter between self and other, Beauvoir offers an account of one individual, Françoise, who lives too ensnared in transcendence and the other, Xavière, who is too submerged in immanence. Françoise assumes herself as a disembodied, disengaged subject, focused on intellectual projects, even though she is very much in the world with others as a bodily subject. Françoise is perplexed and frustrated by Xavière for her unbridled sensuality and repulsion of intellectual pursuits. In taking up their lives in these distinct ways, they both pursue forms of bad faith. In doing so, Xavière and Françoise flee their ambiguity, a flight that conditions destructive conflict.

In the bad faith of transcendence, or the bad faith of being ensnared in pure consciousness, a subject is in denial of her embodied being in the world. She imagines herself to be a pure consciousness, wherein the body is taken as a passive object. This bodily dissociation fails to acknowledge the body as a lived situation, as a condition for transcendence. In contrast, in the bad faith of immanence a subject affirms only their facticity, which is to say, that one treats oneself as an object in the world. To do so would be, for instance, to imagine that one has no control over a personal disposition, say that one has a bad temper, or to imagine that one is defined by a label or title, or determined by their biology. To live our lives as if we are determined by any aspect is to flee our transcendence; it is to hide from our freedom. Taking up one's existence in this way is a form of self-deception because we are not actually determined by any given aspect of our lives.

Both modes of lying to oneself generate a deceptive self-relation and that, as Beauvoir shows in the novel, facilitate troubling, if not oppressive and violent, intersubjective conditions. In fleeing their ambiguity, Françoise and Xavière craft selves reliant on evasion of their ambiguity, and so on a deception of their existence. So, while *She Came to Stay* is not a treatise on bad faith, it is nonetheless instructive. On Beauvoir's account, to be in bad faith is to erode the possibility for a bond between self and other, and that, as the novel shows when Françoise suffocates Xavière to death, can have dangerous consequences.

That bad faith erodes the condition for ethical self-other relations is central to Beauvoir's account of patriarchal oppression in *The Second Sex*. In this work, she argues that patriarchal values codify modes of bad faith into gendered subjectivity. Men, she says, are taught and encouraged to assume their existence in the mode of the bad faith of transcendence, while women are lured into the bad faith of immanence. For Beauvoir, boys reared through norms of masculinity are taught to dissociate from immanence, to become autonomous, independent, unrestrained subjects amongst a world of objects. This mode of subjectivity facilitates the oppression of women insofar as boys become men who live a relation to women as objects. In contrast, "for a woman to accomplish her femininity," Beauvoir writes, "she is required to be object and prey; that is, she must renounce her claims as a sovereign subject" ([1949] 2010, 723). This accomplishment of femininity is a social destiny both imposed upon and taken up by women and it is structured and thus generated by an *almost* totalizing immanence. In a patriarchal situation, women are, Beauvoir argues, ruptured from their transcendence, and anchored in the realm of immanence, which includes being reduced to their bodies, repetition, and passivity. Even if women resist and refuse being overwhelmed by immanence, they are met with obstacles that work to undercut their transcendence. While the more general point of the account of bad faith in *The Second Sex* is that it conditions and concretizes oppression at the levels of the personal, social, and political, the point is that the patriarchal world is a rigged game; in it, women are immanence and men are transcendence. The result is a pernicious intersubjective condition, one that has far dire consequences for women. For in being anchored to immanence, freedom becomes the domain of men.

Throughout her work, Beauvoir describes the ways these patriarchal modes of bad faith show up in and structure the experience of heterosexual love. The way bad faith structures such love can be seen, for instance, in *She Came to Stay*, *The Mandarins*, and *The Woman Destroyed*, and Beauvoir offers a philosophical exposition of it in "The Woman in Love" chapter in *The Second Sex*. In Beauvoir's account of the woman in love, love is pursued not as a concrete encounter between two subjects, but instead, through fixed images—a woman idolizes a man as an absolute subject, while he takes her to be *only* the object of his love. In doing so, not only do they love in bad faith, but the experience of love itself generates women's oppression. Given Beauvoir's continual return to the conflict between self-other as it is animated in intimacy, her considerations of bad faith and love are important. Beauvoir shows us how patriarchal modes of bad faith can structure intimacy and love, which not only generate destructive bonds, but also reveals how oppression materializes through how we love.

That bad faith codifies oppression into everyday life is a point that stands out in Beauvoir's reflections on anti-Black racism in the U.S. in *America Day by Day*. In January 1947, Beauvoir traveled to America for four months, visiting 19 states and over 50 different cities. During her time in the formally racially segregated American South, Beauvoir describes how racist, white Southerners adopt lies to perpetuate the injustice against Black Americans. She characterizes this disposition of whites as one of bad faith because their lies mystify the reality of their situation. In doing so, they eschew their responsibility for the plight of Black Americans. Here's how Beauvoir describes such bad faith:

> Southerners readily say that there is no black problem, that it's a myth invented by northerners: in fact, they're obsessed with it. The bad faith they bring into discussions is proof itself of the conflict of values. Their ignorance helps them; they claim to "know" the black man, just as the French colonials believe they "know" the native, because their servants are black. In fact, their relations with them are utterly false, and they don't try to inform themselves about the real conditions of their servants' lives ... There's an entire system of rationalization engendered in the South, which is also more or less widespread in the North, and its whole purpose is to escape the American dilemma.
>
> ([1947] 1999, 238)

Beauvoir's point here is that individual whites adopt a perceptual frame that allows them to relate to the world and Black individuals in a way that both sustains racism and allows white Southerners to obfuscate their reality. This way of "knowing" is a matter of a faulty epistemology, but, for Beauvoir, the pernicious conditions generated through such intending of the world, that is, what and how white Southerners are "conscious of" their situation, relies on a flight from transcendence. Instead of acknowledging that white individuals commit injustice against Black individuals, they conceal the reality of the situation through a lie about it. Thus, the self-relation white Southerners live out is a lie about who and how they are in the world. This self-relation, however, also relies on a kind of self-deception about the other. "The surest way to succeed [in maintaining injustice] is to convince oneself that the inequality between blacks and whites is not created by human will," Beauvoir writes, "but merely confirms a given fact" (238). In this case, the "given fact" is that whites perceive Black individuals to be inherently inferior. In adopting such a perspective, whites anchor themselves in immanence, in the realm of facticity, not only to establish a lie about the other, but also a lie about themselves, both of which condition a flight from transcendence and the perpetuation of racism. In coming to view Black individuals as *being* inferior, rather than having become inferior through social conditions, white individuals can maintain a lie to themselves about the world and their existence.

What is important about Beauvoir's descriptions of bad faith is that they reveal how we can be in bad faith by living out social norms and by ignoring the sociohistorical circumstances that give shape to reality. She even, however, points out how those who are oppressed can be complicit in their own oppression through bad faith, a reality she describes in *The Second Sex* and in the female characters of her novels. It is true that conditions of oppression can subject an individual to norms, values, and ways of knowing the self and world that can render one complicit in their own oppression, but being in bad faith, or getting out of it, is not a matter of pure self-willing. Rather, bad faith and its ethical magnitude depends on the concreteness of the situation and the extent to which one is ensnared by the bad faith of others and confined by the material conditions of existence. That Beauvoir takes bad faith to be of ethical significance for the way it annihilates the self-other bond and allows oppressive ideological constructs to persist at the level of our personal and social existence cannot be denied. For her, being in bad faith mystifies our situations, a point discussed in more detail in Chapter 6. In doing so, bad faith preempts us from realizing authenticity, that is, moral freedom. As Beauvoir puts it in *The Second Sex*, "Inauthenticity does not pay" ([1949] 2010, 756).

Bad faith attitudes are not easy to avoid. Insofar as they are woven into the fabric of our lives from the very outset by others, by history, by the arrangement of the world, these bad faith modes of existence are already with us; they are already central to who we are. We embody them before we are aware of them, if we become aware of them at all. Even if they are central to who we become, they remain opaque. Moreover, as Beauvoir's work shows, we are often praised for living in bad faith because they reify normative values and dominant ideology. They also, she argues, give justification and meaning to our lives. We come to know ourselves in such modes of existence. We take these modes to be "just how things are," rather than a product of choices made in bad faith. That we are encouraged and praised to live out bad faith means we are likely to be in bad faith without conscious effort. Ultimately, when we are in bad faith, we avoid the truth of our existence, of situation, of the conditions of our relations with others.

AUTHENTICITY

The self-deception of bad faith finds its counter in Beauvoir's conception of authenticity. Like bad faith, authenticity names a particular kind of self-relation, but a self-relation that is always about how one takes up their life with others. Accordingly, this self-relation is not about being true to oneself or speaking one's truth. It is not a matter of getting in touch with some essential, inner core of oneself or attaining absolute self-knowledge. Rather, authenticity is a matter of reckoning with the dimensions that condition one's existence, what makes one who one is, and what conditions how one becomes who one is. Those dimensions are, on the one hand, **contingent** or bound to the particularity of circumstance, and, on the other, **necessity** or a matter of the factical aspects of being human. This reckoning is a matter of forming a self-relation that avows one's ambiguity. For Beauvoir, such a self-relation necessitates an existential conversion. When an individual reckons with how they are situated, they are coming to terms with the fact that their existence is never *purely* their own. My self-relation becomes a matter of a self-world and self-other relation.

From such a self-relation, Beauvoir posits that authenticity is a condition for ethical choice and thus for an ethical intersubjective bond. In choosing authentically for myself, that is, in ways that avow my ambiguity, I also choose for the sake of my relation with others. An authentic choice is not, then, one a subject merely authors to make their own world. This kind of self-authoring would anchor existence into the will of the project and the desire to be. It would anchor an individual in the illusion of pure transcendence. Nor is an authentic choice one that tethers itself to immanence, as this would refuse the activity of transcendence altogether. Authentic choice engages and pursues freedom with others, and this engagement requires an openness to the ambiguity and indeterminacy of human existence.

One of Beauvoir's most explicit articulations of the meaning of authenticity comes from her discussion of authentic love in *The Second Sex*. In a patriarchal milieu, inauthentic love, or loving in bad faith, between a woman and a man, is a result of a perverse self-other encounter. The woman is reduced to and reduces herself to an object, thereby abdicating her existence for-herself, while a man is exalted to a demigod and exists only for-himself. In contrast, authentic love between a woman and a man is a matter of an encounter that allows each individual to exist for themselves while simultaneously existing for the other. Or, as Beauvoir puts it, "Authentic love must be founded on reciprocal recognition of two freedoms; each lover would then experience himself as himself and as the other; neither would abdicate his transcendence, they would not mutilate themselves; together they would both reveal values and ends in the world" ([1949] 2010, 706). Whereas bad faith relies not on reciprocity, but on an elevation of one subject over the other, the reciprocity that grounds authentic love is a matter of two lovers who affirm each other in their ambiguity. Such an affirmation requires that one lover does not posit himself as the absolute subject and his love as an absolute object. Rather, in authentic love, individuals exist simultaneously as both the subject and object of love, and as both a self and other in love. In existing in relation to one another in their ambiguity, two lovers maintain their independence, which is what it means for them to not "mutilate themselves" (706). At the same time, they also acknowledge and pursue their bondedness. Authentic love is thus a relational mode wherein each subject is not only able to pursue their own projects but do so. It is when an individual moves into their own future that is supported by intimacy with the other. In authentic love, the structure of the relation between self-other opens an indeterminate future. Hence, Beauvoir writes, "For each of them, love would be the revelation of self through the gift of self and the enrichment of the universe" (706).

This account of authentic love is telling with regard to Beauvoir's conception of authenticity more generally. To be authentic is to engage in a relation to oneself in the world that neither renounces that one is a **being for-itself**, or an embodied consciousness with their own purposive activity, nor is it one that annihilates the other as a being for-itself, turning them into a **being-for-others**, or when the image others have of you who you are *for them* overwhelms your existence. This is to say that authenticity requires a subject to posit and recognize themself as free, while also recognizing that the other, too, is a freedom. In such self-positing, a subject wills themself free, taking up their existence as a projection into the future, without however eclipsing the other. In doing so, an individual's relation to themself as a freedom undergoes a conversion. To recognize the other as a freedom necessarily requires that the subject also accepts that they are for-others just as they are also for-themself. Neither engulfed in pure being for-itself nor annihilated in a mode of being for-others, authenticity is a matter of accepting the truth of one's situation as ambiguous and always interdependent. It is to take up one's existence in a way that recognizes one's own freedom and the freedom and thereby the future of others, which affirms the constitutive entanglement between self and other.

In authenticity, then, a subject pursues and lives what Beauvoir names **reciprocity**. For her, reciprocity is the recognition that one is like the other, that is, both freedoms, and it is also the recognition of the distance and difference between self and other, namely that the other is always unlike me. Rather than a complete unification between subjects, or a relation in which a subject knows the other completely, reciprocity hinges on recognizing singularity and respecting distance. It is not to see the other as me, but to see that the other is a freedom like me and therefore also not like me. Or, as philosopher Ellie Anderson (2014) puts it, "In Beauvoir's work, recognition is reciprocal insofar as both parties mutually recognize each other as other but is not reciprocal in the stronger sense of seeing oneself in the other" (386).

Beauvoir's conception of reciprocal recognition is a development of Hegel's dialectic between the lord and bondsman in *Phenomenology of Spirit* ([1807] 1977), which Beauvoir fictionalized in *She Came to Stay*. In Hegel's view, for consciousness to become self-conscious it must be faced with another consciousness, thus positing the other as central to the formation of the self. For Hegel, when two people encounter one another a struggle is inevitable; the other is taken to be a threat to the self precisely because it forces the self to come to terms with the fact that they are not absolute; the self reckons with the fact that they are inessential. In Hegel's account, the struggle ends in a perverse relation of power wherein one self-consciousness begs for mercy, exalting the other self-consciousness to the lord. The problem, however, is that mutual recognition is never achieved. The bonded servant is reduced to a thing, while the lord can't get recognition from a thing. The result is a fractured and purely conflictual relationship between self and other.

Beauvoir, however, is interested in the condition of possibility for mutual recognition, rather than conflict, between self and other. She posits that it is from the ground of reciprocity, or reciprocal recognition, that an ethical bond emerges. When I accept myself and the other as a distinct freedom, I affirm that we are peers in the sense that we are both freedoms. In recognizing the other as a freedom, I understand that my existence as a self relies on the other. That is, for me to be free, the other must also take me as a peer. Similarly, for the other to be in the world as a freedom, requires that I take them to exist for-themself. The self must also, however, see the other as a distinct freedom. Thus, rather than seeing the other as an individual to be dominated or overcome, a self takes their similarity to the other, just as much as their differences, as a ground to refuse to the other's annihilation. In that refusal lies the key to individual existence. A self needs the other to be recognized as the freedom they are.

Reciprocity is not, however, about symmetrical relationships. It could be the case that one person loves someone more than the other. Or, as was the case in Beauvoir's friendship with her best friend, Zaza, and fictionalized in the novel *Inseparable*, sometimes one friend is more invested than another. Beauvoir recalls disclosing her love with Zaza only to find Zaza surprised by such affection. The asymmetry in their feelings about one another did not, however, mean they were encountering one another in bad faith. What mattered in their encounter, and what was central to their relationship, was respecting one another's singularity, while pursuing their connection. As philosopher Skye Cleary puts it in her book *How to Be Authentic* (2022),

> authentic friendship is not a matter of becoming similar or of being tolerant. Authentic friendship beckons us to keep

our hearts open and our minds welcome to challenges, to having our being called into question ... authentic friendship stretches you in new, exciting, energizing, and scary ways, but also supports you and keeps you safe because you are recognized for who you are and not for what you can do for each other.

(69)

The asymmetry described here is a matter of embracing the singularity of the other, of not expecting them to be, feel, or live in the same ways as I do. For Beauvoir, this embrace is a condition of authenticity. Insofar as it does not position the other as an object of my existence, this embrace, affording the other space to be who they are, is to cultivate the possibility to avow ambiguity.

At the same time, however, Beauvoir does not think all asymmetries should be embraced. Under conditions of oppression, certain forms of asymmetry are unethical and should be rejected. It is not always the case that seeing the difference of the other is a positive embrace, but rather one that feeds off and into harmful ideological constructs. In *America Day by Day*, drawing on the influence of Richard Wright, Beauvoir writes about how white individuals in America perceive the differences of Black individuals to maintain and justify a gulf between them. "These whites define blacks as the antithesis of American civilization," she writes ([1947] 1999, 353). Although this definition of the other is one that secures an asymmetry, Beauvoir points out not only its lack of necessity, but that it is upheld to maintain distance between self and other and to produce the social power of whites. More specifically, she writes, "The obvious difference between the two castes come from the differences in their historical, economic, social, and cultural situations, and these could—at least theoretically—be abolished. But this is a truth that white Americans, even the most benevolent ones, are reluctant to embrace" (353–354). Here, Beauvoir draws our attention to the way asymmetrical conditions of our situations can undermine the bond between self and other. Reciprocal recognition does not, then, rely merely on perceiving the difference of the other; it relies on securing concrete conditions in which subjects are able to encounter one another as distinct subjects. In an authentic encounter, there exists a symmetrical relationship insofar as they are both subjects, but there is also an asymmetrical relationship insofar as they maintain their distinctness. Such an encounter is secured, however, by material and political conditions; it is not simply willed into existence by an individual.

Reciprocal recognition is not the only condition for authenticity, however. The relation one has to themself as they assume their existence in the world is still key. Cleary captures this dimension of Beauvoir's conception of authenticity best:

> Forgetting ourselves by drifting into robotic archetypes is inauthentic and there are many ways we do this. Beauvoir proposed that some people sabotage themselves by idolizing lovers or subsuming themselves unreflectively into traditional roles such as wife or husband. Others squander their freedom kneeling before an idealized version of themselves (narcissism) or a spiritual power such as religion, astrology, or other pseudosciences (mysticism).
>
> (Cleary 2022, 183)

The point here is that we can cultivate a sense of self in which we forget the truth of our situation, where we lapse into a mold or norm, neglecting to question how our values, expectations, and way of living are instituted or brought into existence. In this kind of self-neglect, we forget that we are each a becoming, and so we end up living as being. We may turn ourselves (or others) into a static image, an idol, rather than taking ourselves or another as a human, whose life and choices are socially mediated, dependent, and simultaneously free and constrained. We may relinquish our freedom to so-called higher powers or by adopting abstract values, and we may lose our relation to the concreteness of the world, both choices which, for Beauvoir, obfuscate that who we are, and how we each cultivate a sense of self, is a human institution, an unfolding of meaning that others have made for us and that we make for ourselves.

When we alienate ourselves in external forces or ideological constructs the truth of the human condition is mystified and our responsibility for our existence is minimized if not altogether eclipsed. We may also live as a narcissist does, expecting others to value only our sense of self, which positions the other only as *for-me*. The narcissist forgets the other as a subject. In this sense, an authentic self-relation cannot forget the constitutive significance of the other. That is, my life is not all about me. Yet, authenticity also requires that a subject not sacrifice herself; an individual's existence is not purely for the happiness or desires of others. I cannot pursue an existence that makes others happy or appeases others at the expense of myself. Every individual must posit themself as a transcendence.

Such a self-relation, although a condition of authenticity, is not in itself an ethical existence. In "Must We Burn Sade?", Beauvoir shows the conditions in which authenticity becomes insufficient for an ethics of freedom. She considers the choice of the Marquis de Sade, an author and intellectual known for his depictions of eroticism involving violence and suffering, as well as for the accusations of sex crimes levied against him. Sade wrote about and publicly avowed his lived experience of erotic torture, refusing the moral constraints of his time and choosing, indeed authoring, a project for himself that he desired. In this regard, he did not flee his transcendence, and in being public about his project, he also made an appeal. Beauvoir's reading of Sade draws attention to the ethical dimension of his self-willing and of his ownership of his choices. She claims that, on the one hand, Sade takes full responsibility for his choices and thus begins to pursue an authentic existence and yet, on the other, his choices annihilate the self-other relation. It is this latter dimension of Sade that amounts to his ethical failure. As Beauvoir tells us,

> Sade's immense merit is that he proclaimed the truth of man against the abstractions and alienations that are only flights. Nobody was more passionately attached to the concrete than he.... Although the greatness of Sade comes from his efforts to grasp the very essence of the human condition in his singular situation [,]... [h]e considered the outcome he chose for himself to be valid for all, and at the exclusion of any other outcome.
>
> ([1951–1952] 2012, 93)

Ultimately, while Sade wrestles with the concreteness of his own experience and challenges social conventions rather than just adopts them, his sadistic choices ultimately neglect the other. More specifically, his fascination with a cruel eroticism was never rooted in a recognition of the other but in her destruction, which turns the authenticity of his self-authoring into "egoism, injustice, and unhappiness" (95). What we learn from Beauvoir's account of Sade is that authenticity should secure and care for the intersubjective bond. We must pursue authenticity for the sake of the bond. Sade's failure is instructive in this regard. Sade may be authentic to himself, but he fails the intersubjective condition of freedom. To meet the criteria of ethics, authenticity must always be a self-relation that is also always a matter of one's relations with others.

Authenticity, then, conditions a different engagement with oneself in the world. Rather than being in bad faith, which could include assuming one's existence through ready-made values or social scripts, lapsing into the desire to be, eschewing one's freedom, or annihilating the other, authenticity requires us to reencounter the world, as well as ourselves, time and time again. It requires the avowal of ambiguity. It is thus a mode of existence that changes how one is in the world in relation to both oneself and to others. As one of Beauvoir's characters, Marguerite, says in *When Things of the Spirit Come First*, as she comes to terms with her bad faith,

> Something changed in me. I went on walking, feeling strangely moved; the world too was changing—it was as though a spell were fading. Suddenly, instead of symbolic scenery, I saw around me a host of objects that seemed to exist in their own right...I had to rediscover everything myself, and sometimes it was disconcerting.
>
> ([1979] 1982, 211–212)

In this sense, authenticity is not a mere introspective relation. The truth of who we are is not inside us waiting to be unlocked. Rather, as we learn through one of Beauvoir's characters in *The Mandarins*, Henri Perron, "The truth of one's life is outside of oneself, in events, in other people, in things; to talk about oneself, one must talk about everything else" ([1954] 1956, 275). Authenticity should be the mood and character of all our undertakings in and with the world. To pursue authenticity, we choose not just for ourselves, but for the sake of how we live with others.

SUGGESTED READING

Primary Texts

Beauvoir, Simone de. 1943 [1954], *She Came to Stay*. Translated by Yvonne Moyse and Roger Senhouse. Cleveland: World Publishing.

———— [1945] 1964. *The Blood of Others*. Translated by Yvonne Moyse and Roger Senhouse. New York: Penguin Books.

———— [1947] 1976. *The Ethics of Ambiguity*. Translated by Bernard Frechtman. New York: Citadel Press.

———— [1947] 1999. *America Day by Day*. Translated by Carol Cosman. Berkeley: University of California Press.

———— [1949] 2010. *The Second Sex*. Translated by Constance Borde and Shelia Malovany-Chevallier. New York: Alfred A. Knopf.

———— [1951–1952] 2012. "Must We Burn Sade?" In *Simone de Beauvoir: Political Writings*, translated Kim Allen Gleed, Marilyn Gaddis Rose, and Virginia Preston, edited by Margaret A. Simons and Marybeth Timmerman, 44–101. Urbana: University of Illinois Press.

———— [1954] 1956. *The Mandarins*. Translated by Leonard M. Friedman. Cleveland: World Publishing.

———— [1979] 1982. *When Things of The Spirit Come First: Five Early Tales*. Translated by Patrick O'Brian. New York: Pantheon Books.

Secondary Texts

Anderson, Ellie. 2014. "The Other: Limits of Knowledge in Beauvoir's Ethics of Reciprocity." *Journal of Speculative Philosophy* 28(3): 380–388.

Cleary, Skye. 2022. *How to be Authentic: Simone de Beauvoir and the Quest for Fulfillment*, New York: St. Martin's Essentials.

Cohen Shabot, Sara and Yaki Menschenfreund. "Is Existentialist Authenticity Unethical? De Beauvoir on Ethics, Authenticity, and Embodiment." *Philosophy Today*, 52(2): 150–156.

Deutscher, Penelope. 2008. *The Philosophy of Simone de Beauvoir: Ambiguity, Conversion, Resistance*. Cambridge: Cambridge University Press.

WHAT DOES OPPRESSION DO?

4

As a 19-year-old student, Beauvoir wrote in her journal that what interested her most was "the opposition between self and other" (2006, 279). Decades later, in 1979, during an interview with Jessica Benjamin and Margaret Simons, Beauvoir again made explicit the philosophical problem that motivated her entire career. "This problem," she said, "of the other's consciousness, it was my problem" (Simons 1999, 10). Beauvoir takes up this problem in various ways across her work. She considers how a self is constituted in relation to the other, why it is that an individual is responsible to others, and how an individual should live given the presence of others. Initially, her concerns with the problem of the other were metaphysical. "I've understood that one can be intelligent and interested in politics; but it is far from me" Beauvoir writes in a 1927 diary entry. "[W]hat price could I attach to the search for humanity's happiness when the so much more serious problem of his reason for being haunts me?" (2006, 65). After the war, however, Beauvoir's interest in the metaphysical dimension of the problem of the other shifts. She politicizes it by focusing on the conditions and lived experience of oppression.

Beauvoir's interest in the problem of other's consciousness was motivated by G.W.F. Hegel's phenomenological considerations of the mutual recognition between self and other, especially in *Phenomenology of Spirit* where he posits that self-consciousness and intersubjectivity are co-constituted or always instituted in dialectic. She studied Hegel's major works at length and appropriated his work to help her describe the

DOI: 10.4324/9781003399995-4

relation between self and other and, ultimately, to be able to account for the reality of oppression. More specifically, the Hegelian dialectic between the lord and the bondsman, often referred to as the master-slave dialectic, discussed in more detail in Chapter 3, is central to Beauvoir's account of women's oppression in *The Second Sex*. Yet, as highlighted in Chapter 1, Hegel is not her sole influence, and she knew the Hegelian dialectic could only highlight a key dimension of oppression, not all its complexities. As an existentialist, Beauvoir's work highlights that oppression is never natural; it is a product of human choices. Historically, she posits, oppression is a way we have chosen to deal with our interdependence, but it is not inevitable. If anything, her work insists that it is in reckoning with the fact that oppression is human-made that we become burdened with the responsibility to live differently.

The political turn in Beauvoir's work came to life most explicitly in 1946. While at the Deux Magots Cafe in Paris, Beauvoir first came up with the idea for what would become her most influential work, *The Second Sex*. Inspired by *L'âge d'homme* written by Michel Leiris and published in 1939, Beauvoir comes up with the question: "What has it meant to me to be a woman?" (1963] 1992a, 94). Raising this question was profound for her personally. The further she looked into it, the more she realized that, as a woman, the world was not set up for her. "[I]t was a revelation," she writes in her autobiography, *Force of Circumstance*, "this world was a masculine world, my childhood has been nourished by myths forged by men, and I hadn't reacted to them in at all the same way I should have done if I had been a boy" (94). She becomes so interested in this difference that she gives all of her attention to "the condition of woman in its broadest terms" (94–95). This personal reckoning with the situation of woman changes the tone of Beauvoir's philosophical work. In researching and writing *The Second Sex*, Beauvoir's project became one more distinctly focused on exposing the contingency of injustice predicated on difference and how realities of oppression come to be lived as inevitable and natural.

Prior to *The Second Sex*, Beauvoir already had outlined an understanding of oppression in *The Ethics of Ambiguity*.

In this work, she diagnoses oppression more abstractly, positing a general claim about what it is and does. She claims that oppression is rooted in a perversion of ambiguity; the oppressor realizes his transcendence by closing the transcendence of others. Or, as she puts it in the text:

> Oppression divides the world into two clans: those who enlighten mankind by thrusting it ahead of itself and those who are condemned to mark time hopelessly in order to merely support the collectivity; their life is a pure repetition of mechanical gestures ... the oppressor feeds himself on their transcendence and refuses to extend it by a free recognition.
>
> ([1947] 1976, 83)

Beauvoir continues to pursue this line of thinking about oppression in her later works in which she grapples with distinct realities of oppression, including in *America Day by Day* where she reflects on racial oppression in the United States, in *The Second Sex* where she considers what patriarchal domination and subordination does to women, and in *The Coming of Age* where she describes the plight of the aged in Western, capitalist societies. In these works, she does not give up the initial insights about oppression found in *The Ethics of Ambiguity*, but they undergo a conversion from the abstract to the concrete.

Whereas the ethical dimension of her work considers how we each must live given the ontological interdependence between self and other, the political dimension of her work elucidates the structures of lived experience codified by oppression and how situations of oppression corrupt the relation between self and other. The politicization of the problem of the other's consciousness offers us new questions to consider: What does oppression do to individuals? How is oppression constituted as a structure of lived experience? What does it do to our capacity to live authentically with the other? This chapter highlights Beauvoir's address to these questions, as well as her distinct accounts of oppression based on race, gender, and age.

BECOMING THE OTHER

Central to Beauvoir's understanding of oppression is the notion of the Other. For Beauvoir, **the Other** names a subordinated and dominated quasi-subject position, constituted by a perverse relation between self and other. In contrast to a relation of mutual recognition that ethically affirms the existential interdependence between self and other, the notion of the Other is indicative of a particular relationship between subjects wherein one is determined and differentiated only and always in relation to a subject. In such instances, the subject who exists *only* as relative to another becomes the Other, while the subject who exists both in relation to others and as an autonomous self becomes the Subject. As will be discussed in the remaining sections of this chapter, although Beauvoir will understand Otherness to characterize a situation of oppression, she does not believe all kinds of oppression materialize in the same way. Rather, she uses the categories of the Subject and the Other to highlight how these modes of existence operate to solidify the reality of oppression, the establishment of a Subject and an Other secure a hierarchy between individuals.

Beauvoir thematizes her understanding of the Other most explicitly in *The Second Sex* to account for women's subordinate status. She puts it this way: "She [woman] is determined and differentiated in relation to man, while he is not in relation to her; she is the inessential in front of the essential. He [man] is the Subject; he is the Absolute. She [woman] is the Other" ([1949] 2010, 6). This formulation of woman as the Other is Beauvoir's answer to the question: "What is a woman?" (5). As the Other, a woman is a relative existence, a subject defined and determined always and only in relation to men: "she is not considered an autonomous being" (5). For Beauvoir, it is only insofar as women are constituted as the Other in relation to men that women's oppression *as women* exists. This claim builds on the one she makes in *The Ethics of Ambiguity* regarding oppression dividing the world into two clans, the difference being that in *The Second Sex* she first characterizes patriarchal oppression as a matter of recognition, a formulation that allows us to better grasp on what basis the "two clans" come into existence. While much more will be said about how woman becomes the Other later in this chapter, for now it is important to note that, as Beauvoir conceives of it, the situation of the Other is generated by concrete circumstances that undermines the possibility for reciprocity between men and women. Instead of the possibility for reciprocity, socio-historical conditions posit men and women in opposition to each other. Men are set up to be able to assert themselves as Subjects, while women are set up to assume themselves as the Other. The result is a perverse recognition of who men and women are. As *the* subject (or the Subject) men are taken to be sovereign, while women's existence, as utterly dependent, becomes object-like. Such a social situation condemns women to immanence and allows men to possess transcendence. In truth, Beauvoir argues, as human beings men and women are both independent and dependent, both self and other, subject and object, immanence and transcendence. Yet, when a concrete situation sets up women as the Other, it undermines the possibility for men and women to assume their ambiguity. In doing so, patriarchal oppression erodes the possibility of an encounter rooted in reciprocity.

This perverse structure of relationality is a defining feature of oppression more generally. When a group of individuals are viewed in ways that condemn them to an overdetermined object status and thus to the realm of immanence, that group, and the individuals within it, become the Other. In positioning a group as the Other, another group becomes *the* Subject. These ossi-fied social positions produce the social conditions of oppression. They do not arise out of nowhere, however. For Beauvoir, there are distinct historical, political, and economic conditions that give rise to and maintain the social dynamic of oppression, which, in turn, feeds and furthers other external factors, such as the differences in educational, economic, and political possibili-ties and status, that establish a concrete situation of oppression. The persistence of these external conditions of oppression natu-ralizes the social dynamic between the oppressor and oppressed. Ultimately, the relation between the Other and the Subject, or the oppressed and the oppressor, is one in which neither subject assumes their ambiguity; the oppressed are set up as immanence, and the oppressor as transcendence. Or, as Beauvoir puts it in her account of the oppression of the aged, "The old person's struggle ... is the refusal to sink below the human level, a refusal to become the insect, the inert object to which the adult world wishes to reduce the aged" ([1970] 1972, 486). The result is that a situation of oppression sets us up to live in bad faith, which, as was discussed in Chapter 3, means oppression sets us up to be ethical failures in our relations with others.

The attention Beauvoir gives to the social and relational dynamic of oppression allows us to consider how it structures our everyday interactions with others and is perpetuated between individuals, often in mundane, more subtle ways. This social dynamic is also always bound to and thus co-constituted by political and economic structures, as well as moral conventions. Oppression is not, then, Beauvoir believes, only an issue of misrecognition. Rather, she understands misrecognition to be conditioned and made possible by arrangements of material exploitation and political inferiority in which the Other not only serves but is also situated as dependent on the Subject. These arrangements are formally sanctioned by governments, say by denying the oppressed group the right to vote or the right to bodily autonomy, and informally sanctioned through the mores of a given time and place. In other words, ideological constructs that generate stigma and loathing of the Other reinforce the formal arrangement of material and political destitution. Accordingly, the Other is set up to lack the concrete means to realize themself as a subject, to assume their transcendence, which solidifies their socially conferred status as the inessential subject, which is to say, as the Other. In this sense, those who are oppressed live an impoverished existence because of economic, political, educational, social, and moral forces.

An individual subject becomes the Other, Beauvoir argues, through how they are constituted and framed by their total concrete situation in relation to distinct, differently positioned others. As Beauvoir states in *The Coming of Age* regarding the inferior position allotted to the elderly in Western profit-driven societies,

A man's ageing and his decline always takes place inside some given society: it is intimately related to the character of that society and to the place that the individual in question occupies within it ... In order to understand the meaning and reality of old age we are therefore obliged to look into the place that has been allotted to the elderly and the image that has been formed of them, in different times and different places.

([1970] 1972, 37)

Here, Beauvoir claims that the status of those deemed old is not a given, not a natural event, but one produced by and experienced within a concrete situation. Beauvoir's refusal to understand oppression and the related differential treatment of individuals as a natural and inevitable feature of human existence is a result of her philosophical position that, as she says in *The Second Sex*: "humanity is something other than a species: it is a historical becoming; it is defined by the way it assumes natural facticity" ([1949] 2010, 753). In other words, humanity is not being, we are a becoming. As such, even if there are factical differences between human beings, it is not a natural, inevitable fact that hierarchies based on differences exist. Rather, a situation of oppression is realized through how we choose and are set up to choose the way we assume facticity.

The notion of becoming is not unique to Beauvoir. As mentioned in Chapter 1, in the history of Western philosophy, there is a classic distinction between being and becoming, both of which are terms that refer to metaphysical commitments about the nature of phenomena. **Being** refers to an eternal, unchanging essence, while **becoming** refers to the changing, shifting character of existence. Philosophers who claim that the nature of human existence is being believe that there is a predetermined way we are. In such a view, there exists a fixed human nature. In contrast, philosophers who claim that the nature of human existence is becoming do not believe in a predetermined destiny or fixed essence; if humans are a certain way, it is because they have become as such because of various forces. On this view, there is no human nature as such, no pregiven truth about who we are or how we act; the reality of what it means to be human is forged. Beauvoir's commitment to becoming, then, underscores that oppression is not natural. It is a concrete situation that has been forged by us. While, on the one hand, this position highlights the evil human beings can do and have done, on the other hand, there is also a liberatory dimension: we can continue to become in ways that undo oppression, in ways that engage collective and individual histories differently. Yet, Beauvoir also believes in the force of history not as determinative of who we are, but as a structure of experience. She does not believe that we can simply transcend historical conditions and legacies of oppression, but we are not merely rolling along purely at their mercy either. We can and should resist them and forge another path.

Beauvoir's most explicit formulation of the being and becoming distinction can be found in the most famous sentence of *The Second Sex*: "One is not born, but rather becomes, a woman" (1949, 13 translation mine). Here, Beauvoir's claim is that whoever a woman is and however she exists in the world, is not a result of her being, but of becoming. In other words, one exists as a woman because she has become one. Being a woman is not, Beauvoir insists, a biological fact. For Beauvoir, of all the things women have been said *to be*—weaker, emotional, maternal, feminine—the reality is, if they are any of these things, it is because they have become this way in a concrete situation. To put it another way, there is no natural essence to being a woman; one is a woman because she becomes one. Regarding the reality of oppression, such a claim is significant. Beauvoir's point is that we can't ground the inferiority of an individual or group in nature. However, we think of a given group and whatever meanings are associated with a group, even if those meanings are lived by individuals of that group, are a result of human world-making, of a sociohistorical becoming. An oppressed subject is not naturally destined to be the Other. One becomes the Other. According to Beauvoir, then, some human beings become oppressed as a matter of living an imposed social destiny rooted in and generated by historical, economic, and political conditions, as well as social and moral conventions, which conspire to trap an individual in the position of the Other. That trap entails confining the Other to immanence, to an existence that cannot surpass itself to become otherwise.

Beauvoir turns to existentialist and Marxist categories to address what it means to experience such a social destiny, drawing attention to both how an oppressed individual and group lack the concrete means to become subjects and how they are misrecognized and treated as object-like. She is also, though, committed to a phenomenological reckoning with the reality of oppression. What this means is that Beauvoir considers oppression as a lived experience, one that is disclosed in the embodied experience of individual subjects. This phenomenological dimension shows how ideological constructs inflect bodily experience and how oppressive conventions get "into" embodiment. In other words, oppression is not only an external reality. For Beauvoir, oppression structures an individual's experiences of their body and their body in relation to others and the world. How an individual moves, how they feel in and about their body, what kind of space they take up, how they are touched by others, what they feel, what emotions they have access to and convey, and so forth are all experiences deeply conditioned, though not determined, by the total, concrete situation in which one lives. This is to say that one's bodily existence is experientially constituted, such that what it means to become a particular kind of subject, or to become the Other, is to live or experience one's body in a particular way. For Beauvoir, then, while there may be certain factical differences in our physiological bodies, such as the color of one's skin or differences in reproductive capacities, those differences have meaning and are lived *only* in a concrete situation. What situations of oppression do, Beauvoir claims, is that they are parasitic on bodily differences such that socially significant differences that justify positions of social inferiority and superiority are perceived as natural. This setup, along with the historical sedimentation of oppression, obscures its contingent character.

A crucial dimension of Beauvoir's conception of oppression is that the lived body is a locus of oppression. Recall from Chapter 1, that the **lived body** (Leib) is a phenomenological term that describes the body not as a physiological or biological object, but as the situation from which subjectivity unfolds.

Or, as she puts it in *The Second Sex*, "the position I adopt—that of Heidegger, Sartre, and Merleau-Ponty—that if the body is not a *thing*, it is a situation: it is our grasp on the world and the outline for our projects" ([1949] 2010, 46). While it may be possible to point to certain biological differences and even, Beauvoir claims, to take them to be significant, it is not possible to ground oppression in them. She makes this point explicit in her account of women's oppression:

> biological data are of extreme importance: they play an all-important role and are an essential element of women's situation … Because the body is the instrument of our hold on the world, the world appears different to us spending on how it is grasped … But we refuse the idea that they [biological data] form a fixed destiny … They do not suffice to constitute the basis for a sexual hierarchy; they do not explain why woman is the Other; they do not condemn her forever to this subjugated role.
>
> (44)

Even though Beauvoir rejects **biological essentialism**, a belief that an individual or a group of individuals have an innate and natural essence due to their biology, she does not dismiss the relationship between oppression and embodiment. Instead, because Beauvoir takes all individuals to be embodied subjects, she accounts for the embodied dimensions of oppression. For her, individuals experience or live oppression in the form of bodily alienation; individuals of oppressed groups become estranged from their status as embodied subjects by being reduced to their bodies. This reduction is a form of objectification that restructures one's status as human. It is not that an oppressed individual becomes a *mere* object, but that by being reduced to one's body, an oppressed individual lives as a mutilated subject—a subject cut off from their capacity to assume ambiguity. To understand the body as a situation, then, is to understand oppression as generating a particular mode of alienated embodiment.

In Beauvoir's view, what all situations of oppression share is how they are justified. This process is one where a social position of inferiority is reduced to an essence. "[W]hether it is race, caste, class, or sex reduced to an inferior condition, the justification process is the same," she writes in *The Second Sex* ([1949] 2010, 12). "'The eternal feminine' corresponds to 'the black soul' or 'the Jewish character'" (12). Insofar as this process of justification blames a human reality on an immutable image or idea, and in doing so, dismisses that oppression is human-made, it is a matter of bad faith. Importantly, although it is not the case that any group that is made inferior is by nature inferior, Beauvoir does claim that those deemed inferior *become* inferior: "when an individual or a group of individuals is kept in a situation of inferiority, the face is that he or they *are* inferior," she says in *The Second Sex* (12). It's just that this being inferior is, in truth, a matter of having become inferior. It is the becoming that must be reckoned with, for only through such a reckoning can a situation of oppression be resisted. While Beauvoir acknowledges features that characterize oppression more generally, she does not think all situations of oppression have the same form. She takes discrete historical events, changes in economic arrangements, shifts in moral conventions, as well as other concrete circumstances to condition the particularity of a specific form of oppression. In this way, for instance, Beauvoir does not claim that racial oppression is the same kind of oppression as patriarchal oppression. They are distinct forms of oppression because of how they are instituted historically, socially, economically, and politically. It is for this reason that Beauvoir works to describe forms of oppression in their distinct manifestation.

RACIAL OPPRESSION

In contrast to her focused treatments of patriarchal oppression and ageist oppression, Beauvoir never undertakes an explicit investigation of racial oppression. She is still, however, concerned with its injustice. This concern can be traced across a few of her written works and her engagement with anti-colonial activism. Her most clear and developed considerations of racial oppression occur in *America Day by Day*, a genre bending travel-diary-essay. This text is an account of Beauvoir's

four-month visit to the United States, which began in 1947.
The purpose of her trip, which was sponsored by the French
government, was to give lectures at colleges and universities on
the ethical problems of the post-war writer. In the four months
of her visit, she delivered 12 lectures, including those at Vassar,
Oberlin, Mills College, and Harvard. Yet, her trip was also much
more than a lecture tour. Traveling all over the country by car,
train, and bus, Beauvoir visited 19 states and over 50 cities, during which she developed various political critiques of the United
States. Like her autobiographical writings, *America Day by Day*
is a narrated record of Beauvoir's daily, concrete experiences. She
sets out to describe what she did and what she perceived, while
also at times offering critical views of the social and political
attitudes she encountered. For these reasons, this book is both a
break from the general, abstract writing of her previous philosophical works, and generative of her more concrete, politicized
writings, thereby acting as a precursor to the concrete analysis
of women's situation, which she had begun prior to her visit to
America. In the everydayness of America, she describes the particular and general workings of racial oppression.

In writing *America Day by Day*, "she did not set out sys-
tematically to investigate race as a site of oppression," political
philosopher Sonia Kruks writes (2012, 74).

Rather she proceeds via reportage and anecdote, describing her own encounters and offerings observations (some
insightful, others naive or mistaken), relaying what others
have happened to tell her on the topic of race (some of it
informative, some of it inaccurate), and summarizing a certain amount of reading she did about the 'Negro' question."
(74)

Margaret Simons (1999) has further noted that Richard
Wright, whom Beauvoir was friends with and visited during
her time in the United States, was a significant influence on
Beauvoir, as was Gunnar Myrdal's 1944 sociological account
of American race relations in *An American Dilemma*. Although
most formative to Beauvoir's account of patriarchal oppression
in *The Second Sex*, Wright and Myrdal offered Beauvoir a way

to understand and reckon with the reality of racial oppression that she encountered in America. She first read Wright's famous work *Native Son* in 1940, which gave her a way to think about how "one's destiny is given by man under oppression" rather than by God or nature (Simons 1999, 148), and she developed a friendship with him in 1946 and remained close with him for at least nine years after. "In *America Day by Day*," writes Simons, "Beauvoir levels an attack on the American system of racial segregation and portrays Wright as her cultural and intellectual guide" (Simons 1999, 147). Myrdal's work was less personal for Beauvoir, but it did provide her with a comprehensive overview of racial oppression in America. The scope of his text would certainly influence her later works on gender and age, but in relation to racial oppression, Myrdal's text grounded racial oppression in social and cultural terms, an explanatory point Beauvoir took to. Whereas Myrdal's work attuned Beauvoir to the external reality of racial oppression in the United States, Wright's work offered Beauvoir a way to address the phenomenological or lived dimension of oppression, that is, what it is to endure and be affected by the socially and culturally produced phenomenon of racism.

Beauvoir's initial April 1947 entries in *America Day by Day*, where she narrates her travels through the American South, offer one of the most direct considerations of American racism. Here, Beauvoir claims, "The black problem ... is first of all a white problem" ([1947] 1999, 237). This formulation of racism as a white problem is, as philosopher Kathryn Sophia Belle (2010) points out, one Beauvoir adopts from Wright. Beauvoir took to this formulation because to understand racial oppression as a white problem is to make an existentialist claim about the conditions generative of racism, namely that it is human action. In this case, it is the actions of white people that bring racial oppression into existence. In the entry from April 3, 1947, Beauvoir specifically mentions how the actions of white people, as well as the meanings and social position whites ascribe to Black people, are the reason for America's fraught race relations. She identifies the white problem as both structural, material, psychological, and as a lived, subjective experience.

Her considerations draw attention to how white people live out the white problem. Racism "makes itself felt in the heart of every American," Beauvoir writes ([1947] 1999, 237). This subjective turn marks her phenomenological approach to understanding oppression; she concerns herself with how individuals come to live out and are psychically and socially affected by naturalized ideological constructs of racism, while also acknowledging that there are material and political conditions of domination secured through the white problem in America. She describes racial oppression not in its institutionalized sense, but in the way it creates a mood of experience, a certain atmosphere that makes possible how individuals are oriented to and immersed in anti-Black racism. In her April 2, 1947, entry, she describes the mood of the white problem in this way:

> And throughout the day the great tragedy of the South pursues us like an obsession. Even the traveler confined to a bus and waiting rooms cannot escape it. From the time we entered Texas, everywhere we go there's the smell of hatred in the air—the arrogant hatred of whites, the silent hatred of blacks.
>
> (233)

She notes how this mood of hatred makes possible a particular form of hostile sociality. "American niceness has no place here. In the crowded line outside the bus, blacks are jostled" (233).

In addition to the phenomenological dimension of her account of the white problem, there is an existential argument about how bad faith lies at the heart of the institution and maintenance of racial oppression in the U.S. "There's an entire system of rationalization engendered in the South, which is also more or less widespread in the North," Beauvoir says, "and its whole purpose is to escape the American dilemma" (238). That system of rationalization is anchored in social myths about Black people. A central myth Beauvoir identifies is the belief in the natural or essential inferiority of Black people. She writes, "even if the physiological reasons haven't yet been established, the fact is that blacks *are* inferior to whites" (239). Other central myths she identifies have to do with the character of Black people as it is constituted by white people. White people's perception of Black people as dirty, lazy, violent, criminal, hypersexual, and corrupt is mythical, Beauvoir claims, insofar as such perceptions are a false belief white individuals hold to justify their systemic maltreatment of Black individuals. As will be discussed in detail in Chapter 6, for Beauvoir, myths reductively typify a group of individuals, and their circulation undermines the singularity of individual existence. In doing so, myths detach people from the concreteness of actual lives. In the case of America's anti-Black racism, this detachment allows white people to encounter and perceive Black people in abstraction. Insofar as it demands a disengagement with the particularity of subjects, this mode of abstraction creates the social conditions for domination and exploitation.

According to Beauvoir, white people ground these myths in essentialist views that Black people are *naturally* any of these ways, which allows white people to be racist without owning up to the fact that they are racist. In other words, the myths serve to mystify the reality of the situation and therefore allow white people to flee responsibility. At the same time, the myths also establish a social reality in which Black people are inferior because they are positioned as such, which reinforces white myths. As Beauvoir puts it,

> Whites can mask their responsibility, thanks to the vicious circle just mentioned: in the condition of blacks, they find an apparent confirmation of their behavior toward them. One of the reasons that allows them to believe, sometimes with a large dose of good faith, in the inferiority of blacks is that that inferiority exists—but it exists because they've [whites] created it, because they are still creating it, and this they refuse to acknowledge.
>
> ([1947] 1999, 245)

Although mostly preoccupied with the reality of anti-Black racism in the United States, Beauvoir also observes how Native people in the United States are situated in this mode of racialized abstraction during her visit to New Mexico. She identifies the exoticization and romanticization of "the Indian," particularly as it materializes through the commodification of indigenous

life. "All along the way," Beauvoir says of her experience passing through New Mexico by bus, "feathered Indians smile on
advertising billboards, their teeth gleaming ... More numerous than gas stations, booths displaying Navajo rugs appear
one after another" (182). The appearance of "the Indian" as
mostly commodity not only obscures the reality and history of
Native life, but it also, Beauvoir claims, makes for a different
structure and experience of racial oppression. The violent hostility that marks the relation between white and Black people
in the United States, seems to, on Beauvoir's account, dissipate
so long as indigenous people generate material fascination for
white people. "The Indian" as the Other is situated as an object
of consumption. "They live a life rather like that of carefully
kept animals in a zoo," she claims, while "the Negro" is situated as perverse subject, for example, a criminal, to be punished
(187). At the beginning of *The Second Sex*, Beauvoir identifies
that specific historical developments result in distinct forms of
oppression, gesturing to the idea that although there may be a
general phenomenon called "racial oppression" in its particular
forms, it does not structure experience in the same way.

There is another key difference in Beauvoir's account of the
distinct situations of Native people and Black people in the
United States. Beauvoir's own whiteness frames her descriptions in ways that contradict her ethical critique of American
racisms. Kruks puts it best when she writes,

> Beauvoir is frustrated by the "Mystery" of the "Indians" and
> by the lack of reciprocity shown to her—even though this
> is surely an appropriate form of resistance to a white tour-
> ist. Indeed, it disturbs her to be considered a mere tourist
> (though this is what she is), and she seems unconscious of
> her position as a member of the privileged racial "caste." She
> is unaware of the seriality that enforces her white identity ...
> The same cannot be said, however, of Beauvoir's experience
> of antiblack racism in the South.
>
> (Kruks 2012, 77)

This difference that Kruks observes in Beauvoir's descriptions
is a testament to Beauvoir's epistemic limitations regarding the

distinct realities and histories of racial oppression. It also points to the limits of her own perceptual capacities as a white French woman. Or, as philosopher Nathalie Nya (2019) puts it, Beauvoir was a "*colonizer woman* or *colon*" (ix, italics in original). According to Nya, who reads Beauvoir as a *colonial* intellectual, Beauvoir's own complicity with colonial oppression affected her ability to perceive, consider, and engage in anti-colonial struggle. In the French context, Beauvoir's complicity and engagement are most apparent. As Nya says, "Beauvoir had many opportunities to speak up about Algerian oppression," but she did not, at least not initially. "Beauvoir's privileged position as a White woman essentially made her a colonizer, unintentionally culpable for the oppression of the colonized. After 1954, Beauvoir's position changed: her colonial consciousness, which showed stirrings in 1946 bloomed and spanned well in the 1960s" (Nya 2019, xx). Beauvoir's tourist expedition in New Mexico makes her situation as a French colonizer woman apparent. Her capacity to investigate her own relation to the legacy of colonial oppression runs up against her deep concern for the injustice of colonial oppression, which she had already briefly described, though abstractly, in *The Ethics of Ambiguity.*

Beauvoir's own situated existence is an epistemic and ethical limit that highlights her own philosophical commitments. Her limits do not mean she cannot *do* better or cannot *become* otherwise, but it highlights the way contingent social dynamics like race, undermine our individual capacities to understand, address, and work against distinct forms of oppression. Nevertheless, her reflections on the circumstances in the United States in *America Day by Day* do offer descriptions and claims about racial oppression. What Beauvoir does at times make clear is that racial oppression is woven into subjective experience and a social fabric such that certain individuals are constituted as the racial Other.

Ultimately, on her account, becoming the racial Other is not an issue of asymmetrical recognition. It is not the case that the white people seek out recognition from Black people for the sake of assuming and securing an individual and social status, while denying Black people their subjectivity. Rather, insofar as the racial Other is designated as so deeply inferior, white people only seek recognition from one another. In the case of racial oppression, then, becoming the Other is a matter of foreclosed recognition. The racial Subject and the Other are always and only in a relation of antagonism wherein the Subject seeks only to dispossess and make destitute the life of the Other. Accordingly, as Beauvoir describes it, such foreclosed recognition generates relentless hostility between white people and the racial Other.

PATRIARCHAL OPPRESSION

While writing *America Day by Day*, Beauvoir was beginning to work out her ideas for what would become her most famous book, *The Second Sex*. In her autobiography, *Force of Circumstance*, Beauvoir looks back at *The Ethics of Ambiguity* and criticizes it for being too abstract. She does not repudiate the arguments of her text but finds that she erred in trying to define morality independent of a social context. *The Second Sex* may be read as correcting this error, reworking and materially situating the analyses of *The Ethics of Ambiguity*. What *The Second Sex* accomplishes is a philosophical engagement with the concrete; it is an analysis of what it means to be a woman that materialized in relation to women's lived experiences. It is in *The Second Sex* that Beauvoir develops a phenomenological account of the oppression of women (Chapter 5 will examine *The Second Sex* and its influence in far more detail). Thinking from the concrete particularity of situation, Beauvoir tends to the phenomenon of "woman," namely that there are people called women in the world, to understand both what it means to be a woman and to end the injustice of their oppression. Her interest in the myths of femininity and their role in women's lives led her to develop one of the central claims of the book: woman is the Other, man is the essential being.

Her phenomenological analysis considers how a world where ideals of femininity, or what Beauvoir calls **the myth of the eternal feminine**, produce an ideology of women's "natural" inferiority to justify patriarchal domination that not only structures, but is also taken up in embodied experience. This master myth works to ensnare women in an unattainable ideal to undermine their existence as individuals. For Beauvoir, the myth of the eternal feminine is socially powerful and generative the normative formation of "woman" as it is constituted and lived out in patriarchal contexts. She exposes how this masculinist ideology exploits sexual difference to create a system of oppression that positions and traps women in the role of the Other. Such entrapment is part of history and mythology (which she explores in Volume I) and lived experience (described in Volume II). Women, she argues, become split subjects, namely those who have the capacity for world-making activity but are pushed into the repetitive, passive, closed realm of existence.

Her phenomenological investigation leads her to draw four primary claims. First, she posits that what it means to be a woman is to be and have become the Other. Second, she argues that women's situation as the Other must be understood as a contingent phenomenon, which challenges essentialist metaphysics that take women to be women and to be inferior by way of biology. Third, she describes how, under patriarchal conditions, particular subjects become women through a deep socialization process that instructs them to live out and embody their own subordination. In doing so, she offers a critique of femininity as it is normatively conceived under patriarchy, arguing that lived experience of femininity as such is a form of existential mutilation. This point allows Beauvoir to show how women's Otherness is not just constructed and imposed from the outside but taken up and embodied by women themselves. And finally, she offers an existentialist view on women's liberation. She insists that to end patriarchal domination, and to secure reciprocal relations between men and women, women's freedom must be concretely pursued individually, socially, materially, and politically.

To account for what it means to become a woman, Beauvoir turns to the concept of the Other. For Beauvoir, a woman is a quasi-subject "determined and differentiated in relation to man, while he is not in relation to her; she is the inessential in front of the essential. He is the Subject; he is the Absolute. She is the Other" ([1949] 2010, 6). Although the self is always differentiated in relation to the other, the difference in the case of man as the Subject and woman as the Other, is that the two are never set up to be peers with regard to freedom. A woman is the Other in the sense that she is not situated as a subject. This setup is, Beauvoir argues, a perversion of women's status as human. As human beings, women are subjects, but under patriarchal conditions women are denied the capacity to assume their existence as subjects. Such a reality makes patriarchal oppression an issue of asymmetrical recognition.

In *The Second Sex*, Beauvoir's notion of the Other is an explicit appropriation of Hegel's dialectic between lord and bondsman. Beauvoir posits that the situation of women is comparable to the condition of the Hegelian Other in that men, like the Hegelian Master, identify themselves as the Subject, the absolute human type, and identify women as inferior. Yet, in contrast to Hegel, she argues that women cannot identify the historical origin of their Otherness and therefore struggle to rebel against their oppressors. For Beauvoir, women's Otherness is distinct in the sense that there is not one historical event to point to that explains how they became the Other. While discrete historical events have been generative of other forms of oppression, she describes the subjection of women as a feature of human existence across time and place, which makes it unidentifiable in relation to a discrete historical event. This ahistoricity of women's oppression does not mean numerous historical events have not been formative to women's situation as the Other. Rather, in Beauvoir's view, women's alleged inferiority has always been anchored to their physiology, not to a singular event that made them the Other. As Beauvoir puts it,

> not *one* event but a whole historical development explains their [women] existence as a class and accounts for the distribution of *these* individuals in this class. There have not always been proletarians: there have always been women; they are women by their physiological structure; as far back as history can be traced, they have always been subordinated to men; their dependence is not the consequence of an event or becoming, it did not *happen*.
>
> ([1949] 2010, 3)

In contrast to the Hegelian Other, as well as other groups whose Otherness was established through a discrete historical event, Beauvoir's view is that the structure of patriarchal oppression is different, locatable nowhere in historical time, but tethered to biology. "The tie that binds her to her oppressors is unlike any other. The division of the sexes is [posited as] a biological given, not a moment in human history" (4). However, her view is that "In truth, nature is no more an immutable given than is historical reality" (8).

The consequence of how patriarchal oppression is instituted is that women cannot call on the bond of a shared history to reestablish their lost status as subjects. "It is that they lack the concrete means to organize themselves into a unit that could posit itself in opposition," Beauvoir claims. "They have no past, no history, no religion of their own; and unlike the proletariat, they have no solidarity of labor or interests; they even lack their own space that makes communities of American blacks, the Jews in the ghettos, or the workers in Saint-Denis or Renault factories" (3). Further, women are dispersed among the world of men, "tied by homes, work, economic interests, and social conditions to certain men," such that women identify *with* their oppressors. (3). Women, Beauvoir insists, live in solidarity with men. Accordingly, men and women are bonded in a dynamic of asymmetrical recognition; they find themselves in each other, but insofar as men set up the world for themselves, it is women who lose. A key feature of the structure of patriarchy is, then, that women remain bonded with their oppressors. Another key feature of the structure of patriarchal oppression is that women do not identify with one another as women. For instance, "As bourgeois women, they are in solidarity with bourgeois men and not with women proletarians; as white women, they are in solidarity with white women and not with black women" (3). In effect, women lack the solidarity and resources for organizing themselves into a "we" that demands recognition. Instead, they live a perverse bond with men that makes women loyal to and complicit with men in realizing patriarchal oppression.

This relational structure of patriarchal oppression is what makes women's subordination an issue of asymmetrical recognition. The deeply personal, and often intimate, relationship between men and women is, Beauvoir argues, rooted in a dynamic of recognition wherein women and men identify with one another but not as equals. Rather, men can assert themselves as sovereign subjects only in and through their relation to women as the Other, and women, because the world is set up for men, assert themselves through men's projects. The result is that women struggle to establish their own projects and thus also struggle to justify their existence on their own terms, while men retain authority over subjectivity. In addition to being preempted from rebelling against men's reign as subjects, women are set up and conditioned to oblige men's authority. This social dynamic of recognition institutes and bolsters men's control over the economic and political realms, enabling women's material exploitation along with their destitute existential standing. For this reason, Beauvoir understands women's status as the Other to also be a materially exploited one. Paradoxically, Beauvoir argues, women experience some benefits to their impoverished status as subjects. As she puts it,

Lord-man will materially protect liege-woman and will be in charge of justifying her existence: along with the economic risk, she eludes the metaphysical risk of a freedom that must invent its goals without help ... the anguish and stress of authentically assumed existence are thus avoided. The man who sets the woman up as an *Other* will thus find in her a deep complicity.

([1949] 2010, 10)

Who exactly this Other is that Beauvoir describes is an important question. Elizabeth Spelman (1990) has argued that her treatment of women's situation as the Other generalizes from a particular experience of patriarchal oppression. More specifically, Spelman claims that Beauvoir's account of the relational dynamic of patriarchal oppression is one between white, bourgeois women and white, bourgeois men, but Beauvoir conceptualizes this dynamic generally, obscuring the ways race and class condition it. Without continually specifying the racial and class dynamics at work in women's experiences, experiences which are diverse because women are diversely situated, Beauvoir's account of woman as the Other conflates "the oppression of women" with a particular group of women, namely white, middle-class women. As Spelman herself says, Beauvoir "leads us to the conclusion that the sexism she is concerned with in *The Second Sex* is that experienced by white middle-class women in Western countries" (Spelman 1990, 66). Kathryn Sophia Belle relatedly suggests that Beauvoir's reliance on analogizing gender and race undermines the power of her account of woman as the Other insofar as it erases the experiences of Black women. More specifically, Belle (2017) argues, "the analogizing of racial oppression with gender oppression problematically codes race as Black male and gender as white female, erasing the ways in which Black women experience racism and sexism – or racialized sexism and sexualized racism—simultaneously" (47).

According to Beauvoir scholar Meryl Altman, there is another way to consider Beauvoir's account of woman as the Other. For Beauvoir, Altman writes,

> there are certain special features about the situation of women, including their tendency to complicity, and the interdependence of men and women given sexual reproduction. She [Beauvoir] doesn't say women's oppression is worse, and she doesn't say it's better or easier; she says it's not quite the same thing, and that it's worth wondering why. Her concern here is not to rank oppressions, but to explain women's lack of the resistance they should logically have shown.
>
> (Altman 2020, 167)

Altman's point is that Beauvoir set out to think through and articulate what is distinct about patriarchal oppression, what is unique about the relational dynamic between men and women, and how to characterize the experiences of injustice that women experience *as women*. It is in her conceptualization of woman as the Other in relation to man as the Subject that we find the groundwork for her phenomenological investigation of patriarchal oppression.

Volume II of *The Second Sex* is where Beauvoir describes the lived experience of being the Other in relation to men.

It begins with the most famous line of *The Second Sex*, "On ne naît pas femme: on le devient" (1949, 13), translated first for an American audience as "One is not born but becomes a woman" (1953, 267) and then in the most recent English translation as "One is not born but becomes woman" (2010, 283). Here, we find Beauvoir's existential phenomenological commitment that human existence is a becoming, not a being. In this sense, Beauvoir's target is essentialist arguments that take women to be women by virtue of biological facts. Beauvoir, however, believes it faulty to accept the commonsense idea that to be born with certain genitalia or reproductive capacities is to be born a woman. Her view is that there are women because certain subjects have been deeply socialized to *become* women. But Beauvoir does not just argue that women are not born women. She is interested in the content of the becoming, and she gives an account of how those who become women become the Other. She shows that those who become women are socialized into a mutilated subjectivity, such that their becoming is not an open-ended possibility but a becoming that turns into being. To become a woman in a patriarchal context is to assume an existence that aims to fix one's existence as a relative, not autonomous one.

For Beauvoir, the social destiny those who become women are expected and often coerced to assume is a heterosexist one. She argues that to become a woman is to be made and to make oneself *only* an object for men. This mode of objectification is central to how the perverse bond between the Subject and his Other is lived. Beauvoir thus posits that the enforcement of heterosexuality is vital to patriarchal oppression and shows how heterosexuality mutilates the subjectivity of those who are socialized from birth to become women. This point is captured by one of Beauvoir's characters, Dominique, in the novel *Les Belles Images*: "Socially a woman without a man counts for nothing," Dominique asserts to her daughter Laurence ([1966] 1968, 119). "Even if she has a name," Dominique continues, "a woman without a man is a half-failure, a kind of derelict" (120).

Beauvoir suggests that becoming patriarchy's Other is a developmental achievement, a "vocation ... imperiously breathed into her from the first years of her life" ([1949] 2010, 283).

She details at length how the social and embodied destiny of womanhood entails learning to experience one's body as a passive thing, rather than as the situation of one's ambiguity and agency, and to experience the world as a closure. The little girl who is thrown into the world to become a woman, to become the Other, learns that

> the sphere she belongs to is closed everywhere, limited, dominated by the male universe: as high as she climbs, as far as she dares go, there will always be a ceiling over her head, walls that block her path … Because she is a woman, the girls knows that the sea and the poles, a thousand adventures, a thousand joys, are forbidden to her: she is born on the wrong side.
>
> (311)

To be born on the wrong side, as those who are deemed to be little girls, means that she is disadvantaged from the outset. Situated as a woman-to-be, the destiny of the little girl is to make herself a relative existence, or what Beauvoir often names a feminine existence. For Beauvoir, **feminine existence** is the patriarchal mode of subjectivity women are socialized into. Insofar as patriarchal femininity robs women of their capacity to assume themselves as transcendence, this mode of subjectivity is a mutilation. The detriment of being made and making oneself a feminine existence, Beauvoir shows, is that a woman comes to live her existence relative to men. This relation is how a woman becomes, or is constituted by herself and others as, the Other. In Beauvoir's view, women are often accomplices to this self-making, as being made the Other because it bestows recognition and self-justification in a patriarchal milieu.

For Beauvoir, becoming patriarchy's Other is an existential, material, and political injustice. While rooted in a perverse relation of recognition between men and women, this mode of Otherness is bound up with other concrete means of domination and exploitation. In depriving women the concrete means to realize their transcendence, women remain in a bond of dependence with men. What Beauvoir's phenomenological account of patriarchal oppression aims to do is expose the injustice of becoming a woman so as to make a case against men's dominance. As an existential phenomenological text, *The Second Sex* offers a rich description of the lived body as a gendered phenomenon, that is, an account of how one comes to *live* or *embody* oneself as a woman, and an indictment of the ways that patriarchy alienates and exploits women. It also is, from a feminist perspective, an appeal that called on women to take up the politics of liberation. As Chapter 5 explores in greater detail, *The Second Sex* opened a path for understanding patriarchal oppression and pursuing women's freedom.

AGEIST OPPRESSION

Like *The Second Sex*, Beauvoir wrote *The Coming of Age* to consider how a particular group of people become the Other. Her concern in this latter work is to investigate how it is that aging is lived as Otherness and to elucidate what being constituted as the Other in old age does to an individual. How is it, Beauvoir asks, that the aged come to be the Other? What shape does it take? What is this experience of Otherness? To consider these questions, she brings a phenomenological lens to bear on biological, psychological, historical, social, and economic factors generative of this distinct form of Otherness. The result is a description of the injustice endured by the aged in Western, industrialized societies. For Beauvoir, the reality of this injustice comes from the bourgeois myths and economic and social structures that alienate the aged. Her aim, as she states at the outset, is to "break the conspiracy of silence" around being old ([1970] 1972, 2). "As far as old people are concerned," she continues, "this society is not only guilty but downright criminal. Sheltering behind the myths of expansion and affluence, it treats the old as outcasts" (2).

She proceeds with a description of the experiences of old age, arguing that it throws one into the position of the Other not by necessity, but because of culturally produced stigmas and a societal loathing of aging. Such sentiments are further realized and entrenched through dominant values and social relations. As Beauvoir argues, "It is the ruling class that imposes their status upon the old, but the active population as a whole connives it" (216). The result is that the aged come to endure a non-subject status. They are barred from existential projects and meaningful relationships with others. To experience old age in this way, Beauvoir argues, is to be denied one's humanity. "The old man," Beauvoir writes, "looks to active members of the community like one of a 'different species'" (217). It is through aversion to aging that "old age arouses a biological repugnance" and is pushed away by those who are not yet old (217).

This mode of relationality is characteristic of bad faith. In her analysis, Beauvoir understands bad faith to have a significant role in the aged's status as the Other. She describes various ways the aged are judged by others in ways that constitute and solidify their place as inferior. By situating the old as Other, individuals distance themselves from, and reject even, a truth of their own existence: their finitude. Such bad faith makes possible the treatment of the old as the Other; for it is only in the perception of the old as a "different species" that they can be exiled from participating as peers with others. Being viewed in this way by others, results in the experience of old age as alienation and degradation.

Like her position in *The Second Sex* wherein the biological dimension of existence is entangled with and ensnared by cultural phenomena, in *The Coming of Age*, Beauvoir argues, "old age can only be understood as a whole: it is not solely a biological but also a cultural fact" ([1970] 1972, 13). In other words, cultural practices and norms are central to the lived reality of old age. By not reducing old age to biology, Beauvoir shows, once again, how ideologies attach themself to and congeal in relation to physiology. Taken to be "no more than a corpse under suspended sentence" (217), this non-subject status of the aged also has an economic dimension. "Society cares about the individual only in so far as he is profitable," Beauvoir writes (543). No longer seen as capable members of society, no longer taken to be productive for capitalist projects, the old experience a rupture in socioeconomic status. In the documentary *A Walk Through the Land of Old Age*, Beauvoir puts it this way: "in our capitalist society ... the elderly can no longer be exploited, as the young can. Now, in this society in which we live, you see, man is viewed as human material, and when this material is no longer useful, it gets thrown away" (2012, 341). The forces of capitalism, then, are not conducive to supporting the old. Indeed, as she writes in *The Coming of Age*, once an individual is aged out of the workforce, they are likely to experience a materially impoverished existence. "Retirement brings a radical break into a man's life," Beauvoir claims. "[H]e is entirely cut off from his past and he has to adapt himself to a new status. This status does bring certain advantages such as rest and leisure, but also serious disadvantages—it makes him poorer and disqualifies him" ([1970] 1972, 262). For Beauvoir, destitution undermines one's capacity to be fully in and of the world, thereby eroding an aged individual's subject status, a point that highlights the Marxist dimensions of Beauvoir's analysis.

There is also a significant existential dimension to the old person's status as Other. Beauvoir argues that aging changes an individual's relationship to time, a point she also explores in her novel *All Men Are Mortal*. In *The Coming of Age*, Beauvoir points out how the structure of time changes, writing, "as the years go by our future shortens, while our past grows heavier" ([1970] 1972, 361). The heaviness of the past and the "very limited expectation of life" in front of an older individual is a visceral encounter with one's finitude. Our existence is not indefinite, but temporally bound. In capitalist societies that equate productivity with a meaningful life, this encounter with finitude is existentially debilitating, Beauvoir claims. "All their [the aged] plans have either been carried out or abandoned, and their life has closed in about itself; nothing requires their presence; they no longer have anything whatsoever to do" (378). This encounter need not be devastating, however. Beauvoir insists that this experience of time is a result of how society treats the aged. "Modern society," she writes, "far from providing the aged man with an appeal against his biological fate, tosses him into an outdated past, and it does so while he is still living" (380). In other words, the aged are barred from realizing projects, and so, severed from transcendence, their lives become anchored in immanence. The result is the aged are condemned to their memories and to a present of boredom.

Although aging is inevitable, Beauvoir argues that it is not inevitable that the aged become the Other. She explores this idea in two other works, namely in her account of her mother's death from cancer in *A Very Easy Death*, published in 1964, and in *Adieux: A Farewell to Sartre*, published in 1981, just one year after Sartre's death. What Beauvoir accomplishes in both works are accounts of the experience of dying and death that do justice to individual existence. In doing so, these works attest to how the status of Otherness can be undone. In narrating the end of her mother's life, Beauvoir exposes the ambivalence, interdependence, and complex responsibility that comes in the face of the other who is dying. Regarding Sartre's final decade, Beauvoir describes Sartre's own relationship to aging and how he maintains a relationship with his projects despite his bodily decline. For Beauvoir, Sartre realized a relationship to aging that resisted alienation: "he had grown old, to be sure, but he was really himself" ([1981] 1984, 136). Although neither Beauvoir's mom nor Sartre escaped the situation of becoming the Other, what Beauvoir makes clear is how an individual's self-relation, as well as their relations with others, can secure or undermine the alienated and degraded status of the aged.

The entire point of *The Coming of Age* is to shed light on how the experience of aging is brought into existence. In exposing the injustice of how the aged are treated, in breaking the silence on the experience of aging, Beauvoir's insistence is that it is a reality that can and should be changed. She argues that it is possible to reconstruct society so that older individuals can remain active members of society. "[I]t is the whole relationship between man and man that must be recast if we wish the old person's state to be acceptable," Beauvoir claims. "It is the whole system that is at issue and our claim cannot be otherwise than radical—change life itself" ([1970] 1972, 543).

THE INJUSTICE OF OPPRESSION

Beauvoir's interest in the reality of oppression is rooted in her concern with the relation between self and other. For her, oppression is a corrupt relation between individuals.

In her accounts of oppression based on race, gender, and age Beauvoir emphasizes how those who are made to be the Other are thrust into "an infantile world," suggesting that those deemed the Other are treated as children, and, as a result, are also forced to assume their lives in circumstances that preempt them from realizing themselves as freedoms. She contrasts the infantile world with the serious world, which is, as discussed in Chapter 2, a distinction she first makes in *The Ethics of Ambiguity*. Where the infantile world is a paternalistic ceiling of meaning and possibility that hovers over the existence of the Other, heavy-handedly demarcating the possibility of their existence, the serious world is a world of ready-made values, meanings, and images that demarcate and maintain the conditions of oppression. The serious world, although fabricated, is a social and historical force that gives shape to the world in which we assume our lives. It is not, then, easy to escape. But as a world that animates injustice in our lives, it is necessary to resist. Whether we do is a matter of whether we can live together authentically, that is, as freedoms in the world.

Beauvoir's politicization of her ethical interest in the relation between self and other highlights not just the mere reality of oppression, but the varied ways oppression is structured depending on situation and circumstance. What happens when an individual becomes the Other is an erosion of the possibility for reciprocity and for assuming our ambiguity. Becoming the Other is a paradox; it is a situation that highlights the power of humanity to make ourselves and constitute the world, but it is a becoming rooted in the logic of being. The serious world conspires against our ambiguity, aiming to fix existence as either the Master Subject or the Dominated Other. This mode of relationality is a charged political matter, for, if we recall the discussions from the previous chapters, if we cannot live authentically, in our ambiguity, we are not living ethically. We must, then, Beauvoir demands, take up the call to end oppression, not abstractly, but in its concrete forms. It is only in doing so, that we pursue a world in which an ethics of ambiguity, and thus one of liberation, is lived.

SUGGESTED READING

Primary Texts

Beauvoir, Simone de. [1947] 1976. *The Ethics of Ambiguity*. Translated by Bernard Frechtman. New York: Citadel Press.

———— [1947] 1999. *America Day by Day*. Translated by Carol Cosman. Berkeley: University of California Press.

———— 1949. *Le Deuxième Sexe*, Paris: Editions Gallimard.

———— [1949] 1953. *The Second Sex*. Translated by H.M. Parshley. New York: Alfred A. Knopf.

———— [1949] 2010. *The Second Sex*. Translated by Constance Borde and Shelia Malovany-Chevallier. New York: Alfred A. Knopf.

———— [1964] 1966. *A Very Easy Death*. Translated by Patrick O'Brian. New York: Putnam.

———— [1966] 1968. *Les belles Images*. Translated by Patrick O'Brian. New York: Putnam.

———— [1970] 1972. *The Coming of Age*. Translated by Patrick O'Brian. New York: Putnam.

———— [1981] 1984. *Adieux: A Farewell to Sartre*. Translated by Patrick O'Brian. New York: Pantheon Books.

Secondary Texts

Altman, Meryl. 2020. *Beauvoir in Time*. Leiden, The Netherlands: Brill.

Belle, Kathryn Sophia. "Sartre, Beauvoir, and the Race/Gender Analogy: A Case for Black Feminist Philosophy." In *Convergences: Black Feminism and Continental Philosophy*, edited by Donna-Dale L. Marcano, Kathryn T. Gines (now Belle) and Maria del Guadalupe, 35–51. Albany: SUNY Press.

———— 2014. "Comparative and Competing Frameworks of Oppression in Simone de Beauvoir's The Second Sex." *Graduate Faculty Philosophy Journal*, 35(1–2): 251–273.

———— 2017. "Simone de Beauvoir and the Race/Gender Analogy in The Second Sex Revisited." In *A Companion to Simone de Beauvoir*, edited by Laura Hengehold and Nancy Bauer, 47–58. New York: Wiley.

Kruks, Sonia. 2012. *Simone de Beauvoir and the Politics of Ambiguity*. Oxford: Oxford University Press.

———— 2022. "Alterity and Intersectionality: Reflections on Old Age in the Time of COVID-19." *Hypatia*, 37: 196–209.

Marks, Elaine. 1973. *Simone de Beauvoir: Encounters with Death*. New Brunswick: Rutgers University Press.

Nya, Nathalie. 2019. *Simone de Beauvoir and the Colonial Experience: Freedom, Violence, and Identity*. Lanham: Lexington Books.

Simons, Margaret. 1999. *Beauvoir and "The Second Sex": Feminism, Race, and the Origins of Existentialism*. Lanham: Rowman and Littlefield.

Spelman, Elizabeth. 1990. *Inessential Woman: Problems of Exclusion in Feminist Thought*. Boston: Beacon Press.

Stoller, Silvia, ed. 2014. *Simone de Beauvoir's Philosophy of Age, Gender, Ethics, Time*. Boston: De Gruyter.

WHAT IS A WOMAN?

Often referred to as the bible of feminism, the legacy of *The Second Sex* cannot be overstated. With initial excerpts published in the radical leftist journal *Les Temps Modernes*, of which Beauvoir was a founding editor, the book was published in two volumes by Gallimard. The first arrived on shelves in June of 1949 and the second was published in November of the same year. Given the shifting political climate in France, of which women's independence was a popular topic, excerpts of and publicity for *The Second Sex* were found in popular magazines such as *Paris Match* and *Elle*. The text's reception was complex. It was initially treated, not as a feminist statement, but as a statement about liberated sexuality and a challenge to the orthodox sexual mores of the time. This early interpretation of *The Second Sex* played an important role in figuring Beauvoir as an advocate of sexual freedom. Over time, it also came to be seen for what it was: an unrelenting diagnosis and condemnation of male supremacy that pushed at the gendered and sexual conventions and expectations of Catholic, bourgeois society. Ultimately, considered scandalous and a serious threat to the status quo, the publication of *The Second Sex* pushed Beauvoir into the public eye in new ways. As she writes in her autobiography, *Force of Circumstance*, she received "epigrams, epistles, satires, admonitions, and exhortations addressed ... by, for example, 'some very active members of the First Sex'" and she was deemed "[u]nsatisfied, frigid, priapic, nymphomaniac, lesbian, a hundred times aborted ... even an unmarried mother" ([1963] 1992a, 187). She was perplexed

DOI: 10.4324/9781003399995-5

by the "violence and level of these reactions" (187). Yet, while this "persistent petulance" only proved Beauvoir's point about the situation of being a woman in a patriarchal world, letters of support poured in from women in France and beyond for decades to come.

The result of the book's publication was the emergence of Beauvoir as a feminist icon. Such status was not her intention, however. "I have described how this book was first conceived: almost by chance," she writes in *Force of Circumstance* ([1963] 1992a, 185).

> Wanting to talk about myself, I became aware that to do so I should first have to describe the condition of women in general ... I hadn't expected to become involved in writing such a vast work ... It is both strange and stimulating to discover suddenly, after forty, an aspect of the world that has been staring you in the face all the time which somehow you have never noticed.
>
> (183)

The result of this unexpected endeavor was the creation of a profound feminist statement that impacted how women understood themselves.

The Second Sex is a political text that diagnoses the reality and harm of patriarchal oppression, giving voice to and validating the injustices endured by girls and women. At the time of publication, these injustices were deeply lived and, still, mostly unspoken. In pushing them out of silence and obscurity, Beauvoir's diagnosis was also an appeal to girls and women to take up the demand of their own freedom. She is, as this chapter explains, insistent that the purpose of life is not to pursue happiness, which she characterizes as a ploy of patriarchy, but to assume oneself as freedom. This appeal highlights how her existentialist commitments inform her feminist politics. The political project emerges from the philosophical address of one of the book's animating questions: what is a woman? This question is a metaphysical one, concerned with what it means to be a woman. But Beauvoir's answer is simultaneously political and philosophical; she refuses to account for the being of woman, for the experiences of women, beyond the contingent situation in which they live. More specifically, however, she considers what patriarchy does to women and how womanhood is constituted under and structured by patriarchal injustices.

There is no denying that *The Second Sex* had a profound impact on the lives of individuals around the world. Women were, at the time of publication and well after, moved by how the text captured their own experiences, giving them a common language and understanding of patriarchal oppression. *The Second Sex*, translated into 40 languages, has inspired generations of women to challenge their status and pursue freedom. As a result of Beauvoir's insights, women across the globe and in different decades, have felt seen, heard, and understood. Without a doubt, in writing *The Second Sex*, Beauvoir left a remarkable legacy.

BECOMING A FEMINIST

In May of 1946, at the age of 37, Beauvoir set off to the Bibliothèque Nationale to study the myths of femininity, her feminist consciousness was still nascent. She did not yet identify as a feminist. It was through thinking and writing about women's situation that Beauvoir would name herself as such. Although initially she had wanted to write only about her own life, the more she thought about her own experience, the more she realized that thinking about what it had meant for her to be a woman was not an individual matter. She realized the world was a masculine one, created by and for men. "I was so interested in this discovery," she says in *Force of Circumstance*, "that I abandoned my project for a personal confession in order to give all my attention to finding out about the condition of woman in its broadest terms" ([1963] 1992a, 94).

In one sense, the timing of Beauvoir's discovery is surprising. French women won the right to vote roughly two years earlier in July 1944, a victory that was certainly behind the times, but one indicative of a social and political climate in which there already existed discussion about women's inferior status. After the war, there was an intellectual and political push to establish a more radical, socialist future, of which Beauvoir herself was at the forefront. A concern for social and political change, which included a change in women's status, was not, then, entirely absent from Beauvoir's milieu. In another sense, the late arrival of Beauvoir's discovery is a result of her individual situation. As Chapter 1 details, Beauvoir's girlhood had primed her for patriarchal servitude of the kind she condemns in *The Second Sex*. In the third volume of her student diaries, Beauvoir describes her personal struggles with the bourgeois, Catholic conventions around love and marriage as a young adult. She is both captive to them and wants to resist them. She is aware that they impact her, and in her diary entries, she even begins to thematize their larger meaning and the influence they have in her life. She later names these struggles with the conventions of love and marriage in *The Second Sex* when she describes the patriarchal trap of being a "woman in love." Yet, Beauvoir was not held hostage to patriarchal conventions as many girls and women of her time were. Because of certain familial, social, and economic circumstances of her life, Beauvoir escaped the institutions of marriage and motherhood, which she understands as conditions that subject women to male supremacy.

That Beauvoir by chance and her own will had different options open to her, was, for instance, a key difference between her experience and that of her best friend, Zaza. Beauvoir avoided and was shielded from certain manifestations of patriarchal oppression because of various factors: she was able to and succeeded in pursuing a life of the mind, she was able to and succeeded in being economically independent, and she experienced herself as an intellectual peer of men of her time. In a 1972 interview with Alice Schwarzer published in *After the Second Sex* Beauvoir puts it this way:

> I have escaped many of the things that enslave a woman, such as motherhood and the duties of a housewife. And professionally as well … as the holder of a higher degree in philosophy, I was in a privileged position among women. In short, I made men recognise me: they were prepared to acknowledge in a friendly way a woman who had done as well as they had because it was so exceptional.
>
> (Schwarzer 1984, 36–37)

In many respects, Beauvoir lived at a distance from patriarchal injustices. That it took her until mid-life to reckon with the personal reality of being oppressed *as a woman* is, then, unsurprising.

Interestingly, *The Second Sex* begins with a frustration over the reality of feminism, not its celebration. "Enough ink has flowed over the quarrel about feminism; it's not almost over: let's not talk about it anymore," Beauvoir writes ([1949] 2010, 3). And yet, Beauvoir spills ink because it's clear that whatever has been said about feminism, whatever continues to be said about it, is not, in Beauvoir's view, adequate. Politically, Beauvoir had distanced herself from the women's movement because, before 1970, she took women's groups in France to be reformist rather than radical. So, when she initiates an interruption in "the volumes of idiocies churned out over this past century" on feminism at the outset of *The Second Sex* she does so not by outright advocating for its cause, but by posing the philosophical question: "But first, what is a woman?" (3). Beauvoir's starting point is characteristic of her philosophical leanings, but she poses this metaphysical question as a political one. How is it, she later asks, that women occupy the status they do? "Why is it that this world has always belonged to men and that only today things are beginning to change?" (10). Beauvoir admits that these questions are not necessarily new, but what is new, is her answer. In offering an explanation about what a woman is, Beauvoir shows us what is wrong with women's situation. Her philosophical questioning lays the ground for her own feminist politics.

"At the end of *The Second Sex* I said that I was not a feminist," Beauvoir says in the 1972 interview with Schwarzer, "because I believed that the problems of women would resolve themselves automatically in the context of socialist development" (Schwarzer 1984, 32). Yet, as French historian Sylvia Chaperon points out, Beauvoir publicly declared herself a feminist during a radio interview in November 1949, the same month the second volume was published. Beauvoir also, Chaperon remarks, did the same in 1965 while being interviewed by political activist and co-director of *Les Temps Modernes*, Francis Jeanson. And, Beauvoir's work as a feminist can be seen in the numerous short, popular essays she wrote in the 1950s and 1960s in which she advocated for economic equality, birth control, reciprocal love, and bodily autonomy, several of which appear in translation in the collection *Feminist Writings*. Even as she may have named herself a feminist earlier than she admits to Schwarzer, it is true that Beauvoir concretely aligned herself with the collective feminist struggle after the publication of *The Second Sex*, joining in the work of the *Mouvement de libération des femmes* (MLF) in 1970.

One way to understand her late arrival to collective struggle is by understanding a change in her political commitments. By 1970, her understanding of political struggle and the conditions needed to end patriarchal oppression were different. During the time of writing *The Second Sex* and for many years after, Beauvoir aligned her political commitments much more closely with socialism than with feminism. She explains this position in her autobiography, *Force of Circumstance*: "I never cherished any illusion of changing woman's condition; it depends on the future of labor in the world; it will change significantly only at the price of a revolution in production. That is why I avoided the trap of 'feminism'" ([1963] 1992a, 192). With the dawn of a new decade, Beauvoir had revised her position. "What I have been able to establish is that the class struggle in the strict sense does not emancipate women," Beauvoir tells Schwarzer. "That has made me change my mind since *The Second Sex* was published … Overthrowing capitalism does not mean overturning patriarchal tradition so long as the family is left intact" (Schwarzer 1984, 39–40). This change of mind allowed Beauvoir to consider feminism in a different light. As she tells Schwarzer, "In my definition, feminists are women—or even men too—who are fighting to change women's condition, in association with class struggle, but independently of it as well, without making the changes they strive for totally dependent on changing society as a whole" (32). Beauvoir continues, "I would say that, in a sense, I am a feminist today, because I realised that we must fight for the situation of women, here and now, before our dreams of socialism come true … it is absolutely essential for women to take their destiny into their own hands" (32).

Her initial investment in the promise of socialism to end patriarchal oppression can be found in the conclusion of *The*

Second Sex. There she writes, "A world where men and women would be equal is easy to imagine because it is exactly the one the Soviet revolution *promised*" ([1949] 2010, 760). Yet, here, Beauvoir also insists that modifying women's economic situation is not enough. Until a socialist movement "brings about the moral, social, and cultural consequences it heralds and requires," she writes, women's situation will not change (761). Beauvoir's initial political investment in socialism as the condition of women's liberation was not, then, a simplistic one. But she saw in the promise of socialism a more radical possibility than what she saw in the reformist, legalistic feminism of her day. In 1970, when feminist activists became more radical, Beauvoir joined their forces, a reality explored in more detail in Chapter 7.

Although her engagement with feminist activists occurred later in her life, Beauvoir's commitment to and insistence on a radical feminism is at the heart of *The Second Sex*. Beauvoir's feminist activism was rooted in a political commitment that lies at the heart of *The Second Sex*: a refusal of the patriarchal constraints—social, material, and symbolic—that limited the possibilities of women's lives. Her philosophical project insists on the ethical significance of an entirely new world. Whoever women and men are now, however it is women are expected to become in patriarchal contexts, must be wholly sacrificed, Beauvoir argues. We must be willing to give up how norms of gender allow us to be and know ourselves, and how they allow us to be in relation to and know others. As she conceives it, this sacrifice is not only a matter of violating or abandoning patriarchal norms, but it is also a matter of creating entirely new ways of assuming our existence. Women and men must become entirely different human beings from how and who they are today. Beauvoir's vision is radical. For her, what it means to be who we are must be completely overhauled and we must completely discard dominant economic, political, social, and moral conventions.

In *Force of Circumstance*, Beauvoir says that what she set out to do in *The Second Sex* was to help "women of my time and generation to become aware of themselves and their situation" ([1963] 1992a, 192). She wrote about the possibilities the world offers women and the ones it denies them. She describes how women are constrained by patriarchal myths, how they are socialized to devote their lives to men, how women evade their own freedom and are encouraged to take up bad faith, and how women's inability to access economic independence, education, abortion, and other forms of bodily autonomy keep them in conditions of material bondage. Through this project, Beauvoir became a symbol of freedom for women. Women of all ages and from all over the world, not just of her time but of future generations, wrote Beauvoir letters of appreciation for her work. "If my book has helped women," Beauvoir insists, "it is because it expressed them, and they in their turn gave it its truth. Thanks to them, it is no longer a matter of scandal and concern" (192). So, while Beauvoir may not have set out to write *The Second Sex* as a feminist, she became one in the process. In her work are feminist themes and commitments that would come to define the concerns of feminists for generations to come. Indeed, Beauvoir's work would become a foundational text in feminist theory, an academic field not yet in existence during her time.

ON INFLUENCE AND FEMINIST THEORY

Beauvoir's analysis was and remains a foundational text in the interdisciplinary, academic field of feminist theory, especially in the Anglo-American and French contexts. Emergent largely out of the women's liberation that lasted from the late 1960s to the 1980s, feminist scholars took to the development of theory that diagnosed patriarchal oppression and addressed "the woman question," working to formulate a challenge to patriarchy's biological essentialism, which naturalized women's inferiority. *The Second Sex* offered a robust springboard for this intellectual battle. Although influential, among feminist scholars the initial reception of *The Second Sex* was largely antagonistic. Beauvoir was accused of ushering in masculinist philosophical and political commitments, often taken to be those formulated by Sartre, and she was read in ways that downplayed or undermined her own unique philosophical perspective. It was not until a renaissance in scholarly interest in Beauvoir's life and work after her death in 1986, that ameliorative reconsiderations of her philosophical ideas and politics shed new light on Beauvoir's feminist project and recognized her original contributions to the study of women's experience, gender and patriarchal injustice. In effect, *The Second Sex* has been the source of important debate and criticism in academic feminist theory, and even among those who distance themselves from her work, it has been no less impactful.

The most famous sentence in *The Second Sex*—"On ne naît pas femme: on le devient"—has been of profound significance. Beauvoir's notion of **becoming** (devient) offered feminist scholars a key philosophical resource for addressing the alleged biological reality of being a woman. While there are various ways to trace the influence of this sentence, Judith Butler's reading of Beauvoir in the groundbreaking text *Gender Trouble* (1990) had a profound influence. In an essay published just prior to *Gender Trouble*, Butler argues that Beauvoir's famous sentence, and more specifically the notion of becoming contained in it, "distinguishes sex from gender and suggests that gender is an aspect of identity gradually acquired" (Butler 1986, 35). For Butler, this conception of gender offers an important theory of gender as a phenomenon that exists because of choice and acculturation. In *Gender Trouble*, Butler turns to Beauvoir's notion of becoming once again to elaborate on the contingent character of gender.

Butler critiques Beauvoir, however, arguing that Beauvoir holds onto an essentialist understanding of "woman." Butler argues that Beauvoir posits a sex/gender distinction in the claim, "One is not born, but rather becomes, a woman." In doing so, Butler says, Beauvoir suggests that one is born female and becomes a woman, which is to say, that one is born a sex and becomes a gender. In Butler's words, this posits what they refer to as a metaphysics of substance, making sex the essential ground for "woman." For Butler, there is no such thing. One is not born a sex either. What Butler does find agreeable in Beauvoir's account of "becoming a woman" is the point that gender is not natural but constructed. What Butler thinks Beauvoir gets wrong is that there is a natural fact of "sex." This critique of Beauvoir leads Butler to develop a theory of gender as performative. For Butler, we become a particular gendered person, but that becoming is neither fixed (it can change) nor is it rooted in any essence of sex. That one becomes a woman is, in Butler's reading of Beauvoir, to say that gender is constructed in and over time, which leads Butler to take up the view that "gender is an identity tenuously constituted in time" (Butler, 1990, 191).

Butler's interpretation of Beauvoir raises many important questions, including:

Does Beauvoir really posit the sex/gender distinction? Does Beauvoir commit to a metaphysics of sex? Given that Beauvoir herself does not use the language of "gender" are Butler and Beauvoir talking about the same phenomenon? And, is Beauvoir a social constructionist? It is this latter question that draws us to the most powerful effect of Butler's turn to Beauvoir. Butler's reading of Beauvoir underscores Beauvoir's own commitment to the contingency of becoming a woman, which is to say that it is not a natural phenomenon. In doing so, Butler's reading of and departure from Beauvoir situates her as a predecessor to the social constructionist theory of gender. In effect, Butler's reading prompted further engagement with Beauvoir's famous sentence, giving Beauvoir's notion of becoming a central place in the social constructionist turn that came to dominate Anglo-American feminist theory in the twentieth and twenty-first centuries.

The impact of the social constructionist reading can be traced to the long-awaited 2010 re-translation of *The Second Sex* in English by Constance Borde and Sheila Malovany-Chevallier. The two translators made a choice to reinterpret the most famous sentence in a way that positions Beauvoir's understanding of "woman" as constructed and defined by society, culture, and history. As mentioned in Chapter 4, H.M. Parshley's original English translation of the sentence reads, "One is not born, but rather becomes a woman" (1953, 267). Borde and Malovany-Chevallier translate the sentence differently: "One is not born, but rather becomes, woman" (2010, 283). In its entirety, their translation is widely celebrated as a better translation of Beauvoir's work, restoring hundreds of pages that had been cut by Parshley and taking care with the philosophical notions Beauvoir employs. Yet, the change in the translation of the sentence sparked significant controversy and debate over whether Beauvoir does, in fact, advance a social constructionist account of "woman." In the anthology, "*On ne naît pas femme: on le devient: The Life of a Sentence*," Beauvoir scholar and feminist philosopher Bonnie Mann succinctly describes the controversy:

> The translation controversy is rooted in the explosion of scholarship on the work of Simone de Beauvoir in the last twenty years, which has revealed a deep fissure between those scholars who insist on reading Beauvoir as a phenomenologist in the existential tradition, and those who understand her to be a social theorist who has little stake in the philosophical commitments of her generation. The latter take Beauvoir to be the founder to the theory of gender as a social construct, and take her famous sentence to be its most succinct expression ... The phenomenologists tend to believe that this is a misreading of Beauvoir's philosophy, and a misunderstanding of her most famous claim. For this group, to "become" a woman is not the same as to be made into one, as if one were exclusively a passive object being acted on by external social forces.
>
> (Mann and Ferrari, 2017, 3)

As Mann notes, the resistance to the removal of the "a" in the famous sentence has to do with situating Beauvoir within the existential-phenomenological tradition. From the perspective of scholars reading Beauvoir in relation to this philosophical tradition, *The Second Sex* offers a phenomenological account of becoming not a social constructionist one. From a phenomenological perspective, the notion of becoming draws our attention to the way an individual's life is mediated by social forces and how an individual negotiates her life and self because of such mediation. Such a view highlights attention to the ambiguity of our existence, that we are neither fully autonomous nor fully determined. At the same time, the phenomenological reading insists that Beauvoir's view is not "gender is a social construct." Rather, Beauvoir's view is that being a woman is constituted through lived experience, which is simultaneously a social, historical, and bodily reality. This phenomenological reading pushes back on the tendency of social constructionism to see gender as externally fabricated and imposed. Given Beauvoir's commitment to the body as a situation, the phenomenological reading posits that gender or becoming a woman is a lived, embodied reality, and not an external construction imposed on a subject.

The phenomenological reading of *The Second Sex* is also an invitation to consider Beauvoir's method in *The Second Sex*. On this reading, the entirety of *The Second Sex* is a phenomenological investigation. The first volume considers the constitution of "woman" as a present reality, of how women came to be the Other, and investigates the natural attitude, the taken-for-granted truths about who women are. That investigation leads to the exposure of their falsehood. That is, Beauvoir wants us to doubt them as the truth. Once the natural attitude is exposed, now that we don't consider "woman" to be naturally this way or that way, Beauvoir turns to a description of lived experience in Volume II. There, she focuses on what experiences are central to becoming a woman. More specifically, Beauvoir focuses on how one's existence is structured by others, by oneself, and by the world such that one becomes a woman in the first place.

In Volume II, the phenomenological reading insists that Beauvoir shows us not that woman is constructed, but that to become a woman is to live a deep, existential injustice. This reading of Beauvoir's phenomenological method positions her as the founding mother of **feminist phenomenology**, a distinct way of doing phenomenology, a way that does not offer us an account of gender as a social construction, but gender as it is lived and disclosed in lived experience. In other words, Beauvoir does not claim "woman" or gender more generally to be a construct; rather, her work draws us into the significance of lived experience, of offering us a way to account for what it is to live and embody as a particular mode of gendered subjectivity. In doing so, Beauvoir shows us what patriarchy *does* to those who become women, and namely, how it harms them.

The phenomenological turn in scholarship on Beauvoir was already in development prior to the social constructionist reading of *The Second Sex*. This turn gained significant ground in the 1990s, and scholars across a variety of disciplines drew attention to the existential-phenomenological themes, concepts, and commitments across Beauvoir's work. Doing so allowed for a different engagement with the content of *The Second Sex*, an engagement focused on the experience of the injustices of patriarchy. American political philosopher Iris Marion Young's famous 1980 essay "Throwing Like a Girl" is a key text in the phenomenological reading of *The Second Sex*. Instead of focusing mostly on the most famous sentence, the feminist phenomenological turn in scholarship on Beauvoir highlights what Beauvoir's analysis in *The Second Sex* reveals about gendered experiences, including those of embodiment, oppression, love, sexual violence, street harassment, trauma, and her feminist politics of generosity, joy, and freedom. Drawing attention to these dimensions of *The Second Sex* shows that Beauvoir's consideration of gendered subjectivity, particularly what it means for an individual to assume and negotiate the imposition of the myth of the eternal feminine, is not in itself a theory of construction, but an account of how a patriarchal gendered situation comes to justify one's existence and persist as a central feature of a social context.

Several scholars have drawn attention to what Beauvoir's analysis of lived experience discloses about the relationship between becoming a woman and heterosexuality. In *The Straight Mind* (1992) Monique Wittig focuses on Beauvoir's account of "becoming a woman" and "The Lesbian" chapter in *The Second Sex* to famously argue that lesbians are not women. Beauvoir herself does not make this claim, but Wittig extends Beauvoir's analysis to suggest that becoming a woman means becoming heterosexual. Sara Ahmed's *Queer Phenomenology* (2006) picks up on this reading of Beauvoir, drawing further attention to the constitutive entanglement between sexuality and gender, especially regarding the way certain gendered positions orient us toward experiences of sexuality. In this sense, as philosophers Jennifer McWeeny (2017) and Manon Garcia

(2021) consider further, Beauvoir's account of becoming a woman discloses how the norm of heterosexuality structures women's objectification and submission.

Although it is evident that Beauvoir offers a rich and revelatory analysis of the lived experience of becoming a woman in *The Second Sex*, many scholars have pointed out the limitations of her analysis. An especially significant limit is her consideration of race and her use of racial oppression as a metaphor in *The Second Sex*. In *Inessential Woman*, published in 1988, just two years after Beauvoir's death, Elizabeth Spelman argues that Beauvoir's only concern is "the sexism … experienced by white middle-class women in Western countries" (Spelman 1988, 66). For Spelman, while at times Beauvoir acknowledges certain class and racial differences, she never talks about how such differences impact the women who inhabit them. Beauvoir lapses into a comparison between women and other groups. In effect, Spelman argues, "in contrasting 'women' to a number of other groups, she expresses her determination to 'woman' only in reference to those females not subject to racism, anti-Semitism, classism, imperialism" (Spelman 1988, 65). Margaret Simons takes a similar view in *Beauvoir and The Second Sex* (1999), claiming that Beauvoir's analysis of oppression ignores the experience of minority women and obscures differences between women, differences that would require a different account of lived experience. Thinking and writing in relation to Anglo-American feminist theory's tendency to exclude and erase minority women, Simons and Spelman suggest Beauvoir's work is an example of the tendency of white feminism to take white, middle-class, Western women's experience as *the* experience of womanhood.

This vein of critique is further explored by women of color feminist scholars who insist that Beauvoir's analysis not only erases the experiences of women of color, but that her account of women's oppression also relies on problematic analogies between race and gender. bell hooks, writing on the matter of influence, details how *The Second Sex* and Beauvoir's life as a philosopher more generally was deeply impactful. Beauvoir was, hooks says, "vital to me throughout the process of my intellectual growth" (hooks 2012, 233). At the same time, hooks acknowledges Beauvoir's limit when it comes to addressing realities of race, noting that Beauvoir treats race as if it only impacts people of color and appropriates paradigms that pertain to race and applies them to gender. Kathryn Sophia Belle (2010, 2014, 2017, 2024) writes at length about this appropriation, pointing out how Beauvoir analogizes race and gender in ways that don't just eclipse their differences but codes race as "Black men" and gender as "white women," the consequence of which is that Black women's experiences are irrelevant. For Belle, "when pointing to key differences between women and other groups, she [Beauvoir] sets up competing frameworks of oppression, privileging gender difference in ways that suggest that woman's subordination is a more significant or constitutive form of oppression" (2014, 251). Stephanie Rivera Berruz (2016) further considers how Beauvoir's analogizing rests on a black-white binary that further obscures experiences that are imperceptible through the binary, especially those of Latina women. Belle's critique also relates to Nathalie Nya's (2019) reading of Beauvoir as a white colonizer. As discussed in Chapter 4, Nya points out the influence of Beauvoir's colonial positioning on her work, drawing attention to the fact that Beauvoir's intellectual and activist work was constrained by her own situation in a colonial milieu.

Beauvoir's treatment of race in *The Second Sex* is certainly vexed. In one sense, this is peculiar given that Beauvoir did have a sense of race and racial oppression while writing it. As the previous chapter points out, Beauvoir was thinking about women's oppression while witnessing racial oppression in the United States, and her account of the Other in *The Second Sex* was undeniably influenced by Richard Wright's account of race and racial oppression. In another sense, as many scholars have noted, Beauvoir is also not an exception to the tendencies of white thinkers to minimize or altogether erase race and its constitutive relation to gendered experience. In response to this critique of Beauvoir, some scholars have drawn attention to the fact that what Beauvoir describes, but fails to make explicit, is the operation of the norm of "woman" and even if that is, in large part, a description of white women's experiences, it is no less impactful insofar as norms influence the conditions of experience for all women. In *Beauvoir in Time* (2020), Meryl Altman offers a different response, suggesting that reading for Beauvoir's account of race and other differences between women is not necessarily about Beauvoir, but more so signals a contemporary preoccupation within feminist theory. With this claim, Altman does not suggest the critiques of Beauvoir's treatment of differences among women are insignificant. Altman's point is, rather, that such critiques might not always address the nuances of Beauvoir's claims. According to Altman, when Beauvoir distinguishes and so separates gender oppression from racial oppression, she is not elevating patriarchal oppression. For Altman, Beauvoir is saying that "the oppression of women is different, structurally different, in that it cannot be traced to a particular historical moment or explained by geography or numbers. But she does not say anywhere it is worse" (Altman 2020, 189). And, Altman urges us to pay attention to the times when Beauvoir is aware of her own privilege. "In fact," Altman continues, Beauvoir uses "'nous; to refer to lucky women like herself, whose battles have been largely won," and thus "suggests that other oppressions may be more salient" (189).

The question of how Beauvoir handles difference also emerges, though distinctly, in the context of what has often been referred to in the Anglo-American context as "French feminisms." Luce Irigaray and Julia Kristeva are perhaps the most well-known thinkers in this tradition who challenge Beauvoir's treatment of women's alterity, or the differences between women and men. For thinkers like Irigaray and Kristeva who focus on difference, Beauvoir's philosophical and political commitments are rooted in sameness. Instead of focusing on what makes women different from men, a difference that can and should be the ground for feminist politics, Beauvoir focuses on what women and men share, namely that they are freedoms; it is securing their shared status as human that Beauvoir insists upon. Irigaray argues that this emphasis on similarity or sameness ushers in patriarchal and masculinist values. Beauvoir's insistence that women must gain access to the realm of transcendence, to the realm of freedom, is a way to say that women must become like men, which in turn, elevates masculine norms. In contrast, Irigaray turns to "the feminine," as opposed to "the human," as the grounds for feminist politics. Kristeva's ([1979] 1981) critique of Beauvoir's humanist feminist echoes Irigaray's critique of Beauvoir's renunciation of difference. Although Kristeva never mentions Beauvoir explicitly, Kristeva takes Beauvoir to be the originator of the "first wave" of French feminist thinking, wherein egalitarian principles trumped an interest in securing difference. This reading sets Beauvoir up as advancing a politics of equality, eschewing women's difference and rejecting the importance of "the feminine," in favor of making women like men.

There has been push back on such readings of Beauvoir. While it is true Beauvoir advances a kind of humanism, it is less clear that she disregards the import of the difference in women's situation or that she aims to make women like men without changing existing patriarchal institutions and conventions. The critique of Beauvoir's humanism also downplays her phenomenological approach to women's lived experience, which is how Beauvoir pays attention to difference. Moreover, as Elaine Stavro puts it in her article "The Use and Abuse of Simone de Beauvoir,"

> Beauvoir's feminist struggles towards equality were neither masculinist nor homogenizing. De Beauvoir sought to improve the living conditions of women, to empower women and to develop their capacities not so that women could become men or compete in a man's world, but so that they could actively participate in the public space outside the home, a world from which women, for the most part, had been excluded.
>
> (Stavro 1999, 269)

Scholars have also more recently pointed out the affinities and shared commitments across the works of Irigaray and Beauvoir and Kristeva and Beauvoir, and Kristeva herself has revisited Beauvoir's work with a more generous lens. Their respective critiques are nevertheless worthy of consideration. Not only do they encourage us to consider more closely what exactly Beauvoir is up to, but they also elucidate Beauvoir's influence on their own thinking. There is no denying that Beauvoir's insights served as the grounds from which their own claims about women's oppression surfaced.

The various manifestations and persistence of her legacy underscore the strength of her influence and exemplify the force of *The Second Sex*. Unbeknownst to her, writing *The Second Sex* established Beauvoir as a founding figure of contemporary feminist theory. In writing such a powerful critique of patriarchal oppression, in investigating the meaning and lived experience of being a woman in a patriarchal society, Beauvoir's work paved new avenues for diagnosis, debate, and moral and political imaginings. *The Second Sex* is an iconic text, situating Beauvoir as a groundbreaking thinker in the history of feminist thought. Reading *The Second Sex* is thus not only a study of Beauvoir's philosophical and political vision but also a portal into an intellectual history.

THE SECOND SEX

The Second Sex is written in two volumes. The first volume, titled "Facts and Myths," critically examines how "woman" has been constituted by the discourses of biology, psychoanalysis, and historical materialism, as well as how myths of femininity define woman as the Other and facilitate a world wherein men's perspectives and lives reign supreme. In the first volume Beauvoir exposes what phenomenologists call the **natural attitude**—that which is taken for granted or taken to be a given in a particular everyday context. Beauvoir's examination of dominant claims about who women are, that is, a biological category, a naturally weaker group, inherently nurturing, and so forth, exposes that such claims are not actually objective facts but are justificatory truths, ones historically posed by men to facilitate the position of woman as the Other. This exposition is how Beauvoir undermines biological essentialism and shows the contingent truth of "woman." The second volume, titled "Lived Experience," is where Beauvoir describes what becoming a woman does to a subject's experience of herself, others, and the world. Beginning from lived experience, Beauvoir offers a developmental and existential account of how it is that women come into existence and how myths of femininity shape women's possibilities. She also describes what relational, spatial, and temporal experiences constitute the situation of being a woman. The descriptive task is a key aspect of Beauvoir's phenomenological approach. By focusing on lived experience, Beauvoir centers not a metaphysical explanation of what a woman is, but on what patriarchal values and conventions *do* to the human beings who become women. Together, both volumes show that becoming a woman in a patriarchal society is a social destiny that condemns women to the oppressive situation of the Other.

Recall from the previous chapter, that Beauvoir understands a woman to be the Other. For Beauvoir, a patriarchal context corruptly structures the relation between subjects. She argues that a world that bolsters male supremacy is one in which men are the only individuals who are situated as true subjects, or those who get to make the world. Women, in contrast, are situated as vassals for men's projects. The result is that "She [woman] is determined and differentiated in relation to man, while he is not in relation to her" ([1949] 2010, 6). Accordingly, Beauvoir argues that a man is *the* subject, or the Subject, while a woman is *the* other, or the Other. This means that to be a woman under male supremacy is to be a **relative existence**. "[S]he is not considered an autonomous being," Beauvoir asserts (5). To be a woman, to be the Other, is to be concretely situated as inessential in herself, as not living an existence for herself, but as serving and fulfilling the projects of men. For this reason, in a patriarchal context, women and men are not equals: she is his vassal. As stated in the previous chapter, for Beauvoir, it is only insofar as women are constituted as the Other in relation to men that women's oppression exists. "[H]er being-for-men is one of the essential factors of her concrete condition," Beauvoir asserts (156).

According to Beauvoir, women's situation as the Other cannot be accounted for by a discrete historical event in which men conquered women and it cannot be understood simply by pointing to men who oppress women. For Beauvoir, women's situation is constituted across time through conventions, myths, and ideologies that ground and propel social, political, and economic structures. Women are given little, if any, opportunities, to *not* be the Other. Importantly, their oppression is also *lived out* by individual men and women in ways that not only elide conscious perception, but that also offer justification for who they are in the world. As a result, it is not just men who constitute and relate to women as the Other, it is also women who assume their existence as the Other.

What this patriarchal mode of relationality does to men and women is erode their capacity to assume ambiguity, which, as discussed in Chapters 2 and 3, is the condition of moral freedom. Patriarchal modes of subjectivity, that is "man" and "woman" as they take shape under male supremacy, gift men the realm of transcendence and bar women from participating in it on their own terms. The result is that women's existence "lapses into immanence," which Beauvoir takes to be a "degradation of existence into 'in-itself,' of freedom into facticity," which is "an absolute evil" (16). "[W]hat singularly defines the situation of woman," Beauvoir writes, "is that being like all humans, an autonomous freedom, she discovers and chooses for herself in a world where men force her to assume herself as Other: an attempt is made to freeze her as an object and doom her to immanence" (17). Through this account, Beauvoir aims to expose how it is that women are constituted as the Other and what their lived experience under patriarchy is, and in doing so she uncovers what stands in women's way, both externally as well as internally, to accomplishing themselves as freedoms. This latter point brings up a key aspect of Beauvoir's interest in accounting for women's situation as the Other: her concern is not whether women are happy, but on whether and how women can be free.

Beauvoir's belief in the possibility of freedom emerges from her ontological commitments about human existence in general and the very existence of women in particular. "[H]umanity ... is a historical becoming," she asserts in the conclusion of *The Second Sex* (753). As such, humanity has the capacity to change, to become other than what we currently are, or to remain as we are, ensnared in situations of injustice. This notion of becoming is also central to Beauvoir's conception of the reality that there are women (and men) in the world. At the outset of *The Second Sex*, she insists that it is an obvious truth that there are men and women in the world. But, for her, that women and men exist is a contingent truth. It is a reality that we have created, assumed, and that we live out. This truth is not, however, inevitable. For Beauvoir, it need not be the case that women and men will always exist. "[Perhaps they are destined to disappear," Beauvoir writes in the introduction (4). Both the reality that women (and men) appear in the world and that they could also disappear is a result of Beauvoir's view that human existence is not predetermined. "[H]umanity is constantly in the making" (44). So, while there are certainly conventions, traditions, and histories that deeply shape us, that structure our possibilities, and situate our existence, we are also always acting on them too, and it could be the case that we act and choose in ways that radically transform the possibilities for who we are and how we exist in the world. Such transformation isn't easy, however. As Beauvoir's entire investigation of "woman" shows, the history of the world and the personal history of an individual's experience accrue ontological weight in ways that work to foreclose such radical transformation. In effect, such histories work to foreclose the possibility of women's freedom.

One of Beauvoir's main targets in her account of becoming is **biological essentialism,** or the view that physiology or biology is the essence of a woman. She believes it is faulty to accept the commonsense idea that to be born with certain genitalia or reproductive capacities is to be a woman. That women appear in the world should not be reduced to a simple biological explanation; it must be understood how it is that human beings came to be women. How is "woman" constituted? Beauvoir asks. How is it that there are women (and men) in the world in the first place? How is it that women exist in the way they do, as the Other? Working from this phenomenological starting point, Beauvoir offers a descriptive account of how some human beings become women as a matter of *living* and *embodying* an imposed social destiny rooted in and generated by historical, economic, and political conditions, as well as social and moral conventions. Such a view means that a woman's existence is a bodily, but not biological phenomenon. That Beauvoir prioritizes an account of women's situation as an embodied phenomenon speaks to her notion of **embodied consciousness** discussed in Chapter 2. For Beauvoir, human beings are not pure matter, and so not reducible to our bodies, but neither are we pure mind such that our bodies do not bear any significance on who and how we are in the world. For her, embodiment is experientially constituted through becoming a woman and becoming a woman is constituted through embodiment.

One of Beauvoir's central tasks in Volume I of *The Second Sex* is to expose the operation of the **myth of the eternal feminine**, a master myth that perpetuates an essentialist understanding of who women are. As she sees it, the master myth is a sociohistorical phenomenon, one created over time through various historical events and shifts, concrete economic and political conditions, and in the context of authoritative fields like biology and psychoanalysis that masquerade as arbiters of objective knowledge. This myth frames women as inherently passive, submissive, weak, and nurturing, which has been used to establish and justify women's inferior social and political status in relation to men. The view of women as inherently nurturing, for instance, justifies women's relegation to the domestic sphere—one that is unpaid because it is "natural" for women to do such work—and allows men to seize control of the means of production. Or, the assumption that women are essentially submissive allows for and justifies conditions of eroticism in which men "conquer, take, and possess," and "Woman is her husband's prey, his property" (171). For Beauvoir, the myth of the eternal feminine also ensnares women in contradictory and unattainable ideals. They must be sensual but virginal, decorative but modest, enticing but coy, available but mysterious. Insofar as a woman is caught by these ideals, the myth undermines her existence as an individual by holding her to a patriarchal image of the ideal of Woman. In effect, a woman is alienated from herself.

The circulation of the myth entraps women into a situation of insignificance, which dooms them to inferiority. For Beauvoir, such a situation is a historical legacy, one that structures the lived experience of women in the present. The relationship between the sociohistorical legacy and lived experience sets up Volume II where Beauvoir describes what it is to become a woman, that is, to live the situation of a woman in a patriarchal context. As mentioned in Chapter 4, her description shows that becoming a woman is a matter of negotiating the imposition and internalization of what Beauvoir calls **feminine existence**, a constrained and passive mode of existence that confers recognition to women. Beauvoir talks at length about how from early childhood through adolescence, those situated as girls are expected and taught to assume or take up their existence as sexual objects for men. She argues that girls are made into, as well as taught how to make themselves *for men*. Women are made and make themselves objects for men. In other words, for Beauvoir, the social destiny of those who become women, of those who are expected and often coerced to assume a feminine existence, is a violent self-making. Central to her account of this self-making is the claim that the imposition of and uptake of patriarchal femininity mutilates women's claim to subjectivity. Rather than pursue her existence *for herself*, a woman abdicates her autonomy and becomes *for men*. This abdication compromises a woman's claim to transcendence. She lives out the realm of world-making, of freedom, only through men. In doing so, a woman also abdicates her humanity. For Beauvoir, this existential mutilation is the key injustice of patriarchal oppression.

Beauvoir insists that this mutilation does not just happen to a woman as if she is a passive object. Instead, Beauvoir shows how a woman comes to pursue, for herself, an existence relative to men, such that she is an accomplice to her situation as the Other. By accounting for how women participate in the making of their situation, she holds true to her existentialist commitments about human agency and responsibility. We are not determined to a fixed fate and that we do have a responsibility for our choices. Both commitments underscore that women's situation as the Other is neither inevitable nor beyond women's capacities to resist. Beauvoir still posits that women have agency no matter how much their concrete circumstances try to rob them of it.

Yet, in accounting for how women become accomplices in their own oppression, Beauvoir also highlights an important dimension of the operation of patriarchy, namely that patriarchal norms of subjectivity, of being a man or a woman, are justificatory. In other words, when one assumes a feminine existence and becomes a woman in accordance with patriarchal norms, one's existence is justified; one is taken to be and experienced as acceptable and worthy. Even if becoming a woman turns one into the Other, such a becoming affords one value in the heteromasculinist economy of patriarchy. For instance, when a girl or woman makes herself desirable for men, according to the conventions in which she's been taught to do so, she will experience herself as desirable, as worthy. She will, that is, receive recognition from men for who she is, and that recognition secures for her a place in the world. Even if that recognition is perverse because it is alienating and undermines her life as for her, that recognition will *feel* good. She may find happiness in it. She may find love. She may secure a husband—the pinnacle of her becoming a relative existence and realizing her social destiny. That she feels this way, that she receives recognition, that she is justified in who she is as a woman, does not, Beauvoir insists, mean a woman is free.

What occurs in this process of justification is that a woman becomes mired in the realm of immanence. As discussed in Chapter 2, it is in *The Second Sex* that Beauvoir uses the notion of **immanence** to account for the dimension of our existence that is life-sustaining, passive, and cyclical. She takes immanence to be one aspect of the ambiguity that is fundamental to being human—the other aspect being transcendence, which is bound up with our world-making capacities. For Beauvoir, immanence and transcendence capture the general structure of human existence. What patriarchal modes of subjectivity do, however, is distort our capacity to assume them both. Instead, in making themselves beings-for-men, Beauvoir argues that women's existence is structured by immanence, while men's is structured by transcendence. Women get arrested in passivity, in life's work that is cyclical and repetitive, which Beauvoir takes to be especially the case for wives and mothers, while men have a quasi-absolute hold on transcendence and are swept away in building worlds in their own image. For Beauvoir, the consequence is that women become split subjects; arrested by immanence and cut off from transcendence is how a woman's existence as the Other is viciously structured and secured.

Although, as explained in the previous chapter, pushing women and men into these respective domains conditions a life of bad faith for both, Beauvoir's analysis shows how the effects on women are the most dire. By being encouraged to pursue an existence in which she exists for-others not for-herself, a woman gets caught, trapped, often with few to no other options, to assume a life in which she does life-sustaining work for men, rather than pursuing a life in which she makes the world. In effect, a woman loses a claim to freedom, and thus to an open future in which her possibilities are indeterminate. Instead, she is caught in a cycle where what she can imagine and concretely pursue for herself are fixed images, secured for her by the legacy of the myth of the eternal feminine as it moves from the past into her present. She gets anchored in immanence.

For Beauvoir, the response to a woman's quasi-fixed existence is a feminism of freedom. Her phenomenological politics tunes us into the fact that our everyday lived experience must be structured in ways that open the future, rather than fashion one's existence and embodied possibilities to a pregiven social destiny. Her Marxist influence insists on the importance of material conditions that create the possibility of living freedom in the concrete, as opposed to espousing an abstract commitment to its reality. Her existentialism is a reminder that at the heart of her feminist politics is a commitment to living authentically, which, as Chapter 3 details, means living an existence in which the self and other assume their ambiguity. Each of these realities is undermined by patriarchal oppression.

The work of liberation is not easy, Beauvoir claims. Insofar as women's situation as the Other, as relative to men, as objects for men, is lived out pre-reflectively and structurally, and are historically sedimented realities, they cannot be interrupted by formal measures alone. They must also be interrupted at the unconscious, embodied layers of our existence. Moreover, because it requires refusing and ultimately sacrificing norms and customs of femininity and masculinity, the very ones that are, for many, sources of happiness and self-justification, the work of liberation will cause conflict. Liberation is also not a matter of appealing to men to give women freedom; it is very much a matter of women discovering their solidarity, rejecting the bad faith temptations of happiness and discovering the pleasures of struggling for their own freedom. While Beauvoir alerts us to the tensions and conflicts that this will create between men and women, she does not envision a permanent state of hostility. What she does insist on, however, is that both men and women must commit to sacrificing patriarchal myths. This sacrifice does not amount to men and women becoming the same, however. She does not advocate for pure equality nor the affirmation of pure difference between men and women. Rather, she insists that all human beings must have the capacity to assume themselves as freedom.

Her appeal to the freedom of all human beings does not collapse into a form of liberal humanism wherein all individuals are understood to be the same. There will still be physiological differences, even in the absence of patriarchal oppression. Unlike today, however, these differences will appear in new ways. They will take on new meanings. They will not be used to justify the difference between a Subject and his Inessential Other. Ultimately, according to her, the goal of liberation is our mutual recognition of each other as free, in our distinctness and in relation to one another. To realize this, there must be a complete overhaul of patriarchal morality, affective dispositions, and customs that demand girls' and women's passivity and deny them their bodily autonomy. In short, the myth of the eternal feminine must be dismantled. So long as it prevails, economic and political advances will fall short of the goal of liberation.

UNDOING THE BONDS OF PATRIARCHY

Controversial from the start, *The Second Sex* has inspired generations to diagnose and challenge women's inferior status. It has and continues to give voice to the injustices lived by those who are or are taken to be girls and women and continues to be a vehicle for feminist visions of social, moral, and political liberation. By imposing a social destiny onto women, by denying women freedom, patriarchy robs all of us of the capacity to undertake ethical relations with others and with ourselves. For Beauvoir, the collective response must be a feminism of freedom. Without the collective pursuit of freedom, not in the liberal sense of doing as one pleases, but in the sense of opening and holding open a future of indeterminate possibilities, patriarchal injustices will persist. We will continue to live out the limited and morally corrupt possibilities patriarchy offers. Individually and collectively, we will remain in an unethical bond, one in which the self-other relation will continue to suffer.

At the end of *The Second Sex*, Beauvoir insists on the pursuit of freedom. What must be achieved is not women's independence, but freedom in the moral sense. *The Second Sex* is, then, an appeal to take a politics of freedom not merely at the level of formal equality, but also in how we assume ourselves and our relations with others. As Beauvoir explains in *The Ethics of Ambiguity*, and as Chapter 2 highlights, the success of any appeal is the extent to which others take it up. What we must do, Beauvoir insists, is undo the bonds of patriarchy. Only then will we be able to pursue our becoming authentically.

SUGGESTED READING

Primary Texts

Beauvoir, Simone de. 1949. *Le Deuxième Sexe*. Paris: Gallimard.

——— 1953. *The Second Sex*. Translated by H.M. Pashley. New York: Knopf.

——— 2010. *The Second Sex*. Translated by C. Borde and S. Malovany-Chevallier. New York: Alfred A. Knopf.

——— 2015. *Feminist Writings*. Edited by M.A. Simons and M.B. Timmerman. Urbana: University of Illinois Press.

Secondary Texts

Ahmed, Sara. 2006. *Queer Phenomenology*. Durham and London: Duke University Press.

Altman, Meryl. 2020. *Beauvoir in Time*. Leiden, The Netherlands: Brill.

Bauer, Nancy, 2001. *Simone de Beauvoir, Philosophy, and Feminism*. New York: Columbia University Press.

Belle, Kathryn Sophia. 2010. "Sartre, Beauvoir, and the Race/Gender Analogy: A Case for Black Feminist Philosophy." In *Convergences: Black Feminism and Continental Philosophy*, edited by Donna-Dale L. Marcano, Kathryn T. Gines (now Belle), and Maria del Guadalupe, 35–51. Albany: SUNY Press.

————— 2014. "Comparative and Competing Frameworks of Oppression in Simone de Beauvoir's The Second Sex." *Graduate Faculty Philosophy Journal*, 35(1–2): 251–273.

————— 2017. "Simone de Beauvoir and the Race/Gender Analogy in The Second Sex Revisited." In *A Companion to Simone de Beauvoir*, edited by Laura Hengehold and Nancy Bauer, 47–58. New York: Wiley.

————— 2024. *Beauvoir and Belle: A Black Feminist Critique of* The Second Sex. Oxford: Oxford University Press.

Bergoffen, Debra. 1997. *The Philosophy of Simone de Beauvoir: Gendered Phenomenologies, Erotic Generosities*. Albany, NY: State University of New York Press.

Berruz, Stephanie Rivera. 2016. "At the Crossroads: Latina Identity and Simone de Beauvoir's *The Second Sex*." *Hypatia*, 31(2): 319–333.

Butler, Judith. 1986. "Sex and Gender in Simone de Beauvoir's The Second Sex." *Yale French Studies*. 72: 35–49.

————— 1990. *Gender Trouble: Feminism and the Subversion of Identity*. New York: Routledge.

Garcia, Manon, [2018] 2021. *We Are Not Born Submissive: How Patriarchy Shapes Women's Lives*. Princeton: Princeton University Press.

hooks, bell. 2012. "True Philosophers: Beauvoir and bell." In *Beauvoir and Western Thought from Plato to Butler*, edited by Shannon M. Mussett and William S. Wilkerson, 227–236. Albany: SUNY Press.

Kristeva, Julia. [1979] 1981. "Women's Time." Translated by Alice Jardine and Harry Blake. *Signs* 7(11): 7–35

Mann, Bonnie and Martina Ferrari, eds. 2017. "*On ne naît pas femme: on le devient …*" The Life of a Sentence. Oxford: Oxford University Press.

McWeeny, Jennifer. 2017. "The Second Sex of Consciousness: A New Ontology and Temporality for Beauvoir's 'Becoming a Woman.'" In "*On ne naît pas femme: on le devient …*" *The Life of a Sentence*, edited by Bonnie Mann and Martina Ferrari, 231–274. Oxford: Oxford University Press.

Moi, Toril. 1990. *Feminist Theory and Simone de Beauvoir*. Oxford and Cambridge: Blackwell.

Nya, Nathalie. 2019. *Simone de Beauvoir and the Colonial Experience: Freedom, Violence, and Identity*. Lanham: Lexington Books.

Schwarzer, Alice. 1984. *After "The Second Sex": Conversations with Simone de Beauvoir*. New York: Pantheon Books.

Simons, Margaret. 1983. "The Silencing of Simone de Beauvoir: Guess What's Missing from The Second Sex." *Women's Studies International Forum*. 6(5): 559–564.

———— 1990. "Sexism and the Philosophical Canon: On Reading Beauvoir's The Second Sex." *Journal of the History of Ideas* 51(3): 487–504.

———— 1999. *Beauvoir and "The Second Sex": Feminism, Race, and the Origins of Existentialism*. Lanham: Rowman and Littlefield.

Spelman, Elizabeth V. 1988. "Simone de Beauvoir: Just Who Does She Think 'We' Is?" In *Inessential Woman: Problems of Exclusion in Feminist Thought*, 57–79, Boston: Beacon Press.

Wittig, Monique. [1980] 1981. "One is Not Born a Woman." *Feminist Issues* 1(2):47–54.

Young, Iris Marion. 1980. "Throwing Like a Girl: A Phenomenology of Feminine Body Comportment, Motility, and Spatiality." *Human Studies*, 3: 137–156.

6

HOW DO WE END OPPRESSION?

Although Beauvoir describes the time after World War II as the moral period of her work, there is an undeniable political bend to her postwar writings. Her experience of the war prompted a shift in her thinking, as well as in her attitude toward and orientation in the world. The moral period was thus also characterized by an explicit politicization of her thinking, was attuned to the concrete, to the ways the co-mingling of historical events, social structures, and personal experiences are generative of and work upon the lived, embodied possibility of being free with others in the world. This period makes explicit that to think the self-other relation always requires thinking about the moral and political dimensions of existence, for these dimensions are not only inextricable from who we are, but they are also the locus of the possibility of our freedom. As Chapters 4 and 5 highlight, instead of focusing on the conditions of our happiness, Beauvoir was most concerned with how realities of oppression interrupt authentic freedom, or what she called **moral freedom**.

Chapter 2 accounts for how this conception of freedom offers an alternative to a conception of radical freedom as an ontological condition. It is possible, though, to characterize Beauvoir's notion of moral freedom as radical in a different sense. Her conception of freedom demands a commitment to addressing the concrete conditions and ways of living that conspire against it. In effect, her work doesn't just offer a rich description of the realities and structures of oppression, she also offers a distinct answer to the question: how do we end

DOI: 10.4324/9781003399995-6

oppression? Beauvoir's response is a grounded, material vision of solidarity committed to the struggle against oppression and the pursuit of political emancipation. Importantly, Beauvoir's commitment to emancipation is not merely existential; it can only be achieved if it is concretely secured by social and material conditions.

For Beauvoir, silence about and complicity with oppression are just as problematic as active participation in it. The passivity of apolitical dispositions, as well as the passivity of going along with the world as it is, constitutes an evil, even if distinct from those who authorize and practice violence and torture and who intentionally uphold social structures that hinder the freedom of certain individuals and groups. In *Useless Mouths*, Beauvoir's only play, she underscores the significance of not turning one's back on the material and political conditions of the world. For her, to be able to cut oneself off from the realities of oppression others face is indicative of a situation of privilege. To cut oneself off from the world as Jean-Pierre does in the city of Vaucelles while women and children are discarded is to abdicate one's responsibility for the world as it is; his abdication is a condition of their oppression. When he comes to terms with the evil he conspires with, he admits that the love of the other who endures oppression is a political relation. To love the other who is oppressed demands that he, too, struggles against the concrete reality of oppression. When Jean-Pierre asserts, "We struggle together," he is affirming not just an ethical bond between self and other but creating a bond of political solidarity. For Beauvoir, that gesture is one we all must make in the face of oppression. It is the only way to transform the relation between those who are privileged and those who are oppressed. It is the only way to transform the material conditions of oppression—the conditions that keep some people poor, hungry, and without shelter, that push some people closer to death, that subject some people to forms of torture and annihilation.

Beauvoir did not just envision what it means to achieve social and political change. As the final chapter of this book shows, she also put her vision into practice, using the power of her pen to draw attention to the realities of oppression and to call out complicity. At various times in her life, Beauvoir used her status and privilege as a well-known, white French intellectual to insist on the moral urgency of struggling together. Beauvoir, however, knew that much stood in the way of realizing solidarity. Influenced in large part by Marx, Beauvoir was interested in phenomena and forms of relationality that obscure or mask the social and material conditions that secure and perpetuate oppression. For Beauvoir, even if oppression is in plain sight, there are social forces that justify and thereby conceal its reality. Mystifying phenomena, she shows us, structure our lived experience and often make us complicit in oppression, including our own. Our experience of mystification limits and forecloses our capacity to feel and act in ways that challenge oppression, that obstruct solidarity, and ultimately preempt social and political change. To understand how to end oppression, we must also, Beauvoir insists, consider how mystification operates in our lives. In addition to accounting for Beauvoir's conception of solidarity, this chapter thus also underscores her consideration of phenomena that obscure individual and collective political change.

ON SOCIAL AND POLITICAL CHANGE

As discussed in more detail in Chapter 1, the changing social and political climate of World War II played a major role in inaugurating the moral period of her work. As the war progressed, Beauvoir's attention shifted from a focus on the self's struggle with the other to a concern for the way social and political structures and events mediate one's existence and possibilities. This conversion is central to her development of an account of situated subjectivity, or as she puts it in the January 2, 1940, entry from her *Wartime Diary*, an "individualist life but penetrated as much as possible by the social" ([1990] 2009, 20). Through her study of Hegel during this time, she became increasingly interested in the relation between the individual and the force of history. When she turned to Kierkegaard in 1940, Beauvoir is drawn to his considerations of anguish and courage as she is confronted with the realities of French collaboration and the violence of Nazi occupation. Her entries in *Wartime Diary*, published *Letters to Sartre*, as well as her reflections in *The Prime of Life*, also speak to this conversion. When she confronted the war in more personal ways – her lovers Jacques Bost was on the front lines and Sartre was held for nine months as a prison of war – Beauvoir became overwhelmed with distress and guilt. When she considered her position as an intellectual and the possibility of active and passive collaboration with the Nazis she became increasingly concerned with how individuals evaded, consciously or not, its injustice.

In *The Prime of Life*, the second volume of her autobiography that details the years from 1929 to 1944, Beauvoir accounts for the change in her disposition. In an important passage that highlights the moral and political bend of the conversion, she writes:

> I already knew that in the very marrow of my being I was bound up with my contemporaries; now I was learning that this dependent condition carried a complementary burden of responsibility … My salvation was bound up with that of my country as a whole. But I myself, as I learned from my guilt and remorse, had been partially responsible for creating the situation now forced upon me.
>
> ([1960] 1962, 358)

Beauvoir's personal confrontation with the situation imposed on her by war, one that she does not absolve herself of responsibility for participating in, was a catalyst for a transformation in her thinking. It's no wonder, then, that around 1940 Beauvoir began to develop an account of freedom as situated and contingent. In large part, it was the reality of war that made her "abandon the plane of the individual, and therefore idealistic, morality" on which she had committed herself to prior (346).

It wasn't the war that made her realize the constitutive entanglement between self and other, however. As is clear in her early novels, she already grasped this metaphysical truth. Rather, in the face and wake of the war, she began to reckon with the moral and political dimensions of subjectivity. Her diary entry from January 21, 1941 in the *Wartime Diary* speaks to this clearly: "My novel [*She Came to Stay*]. I'm eager to finish it. It rests on a philosophical attitude that is already no longer mine. My next novel will be about *the individual situation*, its moral significance and its relation to the social" ([1990] 2009, 320). In that same entry, Beauvoir rejects her prior preoccupation with happiness, noting that it is an introspective ideal. Years later in *The Second Sex*, Beauvoir denounces the pursuit of happiness as a viable political project:

> We cannot really know what "happiness" means, and still less what authentic values it covers; there is no way to measure the happiness of others, and it is always easy to call a situation that one would like to impose on others happy: in particular, we declare happy those condemned to stagnation, under the pretext of happiness is immobility. This is a notion, then, we will not refer to.
>
> ([1949] 2010, 16)

Instead of happiness, Beauvoir's concern is with the social and material conditions that secure freedom.

Amidst wartime, and even as she confronted the weight of responsibility, Beauvoir, like many individuals of her time, did not immediately take political action. She found herself overwhelmed by the reality of the war and, as a result, unable to grasp the possibility of her agency. As German troops occupied Paris, as her lovers and friends were sent off to service, as she witnessed and confronted history moving in, Beauvoir became engulfed in passivity, characterized by waiting. She spent her time waiting to receive letters from Sartre, caught up in despair in the meantime. At the same time, she also describes the experience of waiting as depersonalized. "I am ... waiting for I don't know what. It seems that everyone is waiting, as if pure time had any efficacy," Beauvoir writes in a diary entry from October 3, 1939 ([1990] 2009, 85). What Beauvoir comes to realize is that this experience of waiting is conditioned by the situation of war. It is not inevitable, but a matter of being overcome by history as it pushes and presses on individual and collective life. Although preemptive of political action, this experience speaks to Beauvoir's concern with complicity and passivity in the face of history and injustice. Her struggles to write, to act, were not a matter of destiny, but a result of the force of circumstance.

In the face of the German Occupation, Beauvoir struggled to assume herself as an individual and to see the possibility for political recourse. In *The Prime of Life*, she recounts feeling shocked by Sartre's attitude upon his return to Paris after his time as a prisoner of war. "He had not come back to enjoy the sweets of freedom ..." ([1960] 1962, 381). Beauvoir writes, "but to *act*. How? I inquired, taken aback. We were so isolated, so powerless! It was precisely this isolation that had to be broken down, he said. We had to unite, to organize a resistance movement. I remained skeptical" (381). Even though initially overwhelmed by the reality of the war, Beauvoir came to participate in political efforts, forming, alongside Sartre and other French intellectuals, "Socialisme et Liberté," which distributed information to support the resistance movement.

Beauvoir's politics, as the next chapter shows, were occasionally complicated and problematic, but she did not shy away from the importance of political action. In fact, in her first postwar philosophical essay "Pyrrhus and Cineas," published in 1944, Beauvoir discusses the moral significance of political action. There, and later in *The Ethics of Ambiguity*, Beauvoir accounts for the moral dimension of political action. For her, the guiding value of all political action is freedom, but not in the abstract, individualistic, or entitled sense. Political action should cultivate conditions of freedom concretely. In "Pyrrhus and Cineas," Beauvoir is clear that her conception of political action is not about creating equality. What matters to her is securing material conditions for all individuals that allow them to pursue **projects**, or world-building activity. We must work for "health, knowledge, well-being, and leisure for all men so that their freedom is not consumed in fighting sickness, ignorance, and misery" ([1944] 2004, 137). In other words, the goal of political action should not be to make people the same, but to create social and material conditions that allow each individual to pursue world-building, transcendent activity. Political efforts that do not pursue or that work to undermine such a possibility are, on Beauvoir's account, morally corrupt.

Her conception of political action is not, however, idealistic. As political philosopher Sonia Kruks remarks, "Beauvoir criticizes political decisions made on *a priori* grounds" (Kruks 2012, 42). For Beauvoir, political decisions and action must be based on the specificity and particularity of a given circumstance, not on a pre-given ideal about what must occur. There are no pure political ideals, she argues. To claim, for instance, that peace is always, no matter what, the right course of action is bad faith. So, too, would the claim that revenge is always justifiable. For Beauvoir, political action must be based on the concrete givens. While in one instance non-violence may be the right course of political action, in another violence may be necessary, but we cannot *a priori*, that is, before the situation at hand, know what is right to do. On this basis, Beauvoir challenges the abstract, universalism of Kantian ethics. "We must define *our* own good," Beauvoir writes in "Pyrrhus and Cineas" in critique of Kant ([1944] 2004, 127). "The respect of the human person in general cannot suffice to guide us because we are dealing with separate and oppressed individuals" (127).

This conception of political action can even be found in her novel, *All Men are Mortal* (1946). Although it is not a story about World War II and most certainly an existential account of how existence is finite, the main character, Fosca, a political leader, is confronted with the horrors of political action that is unresponsive to the concrete circumstances of life. What Fosca does not do as a political leader, but his grandson Armand does, is undertake action rooted in the concrete possibilities of the present. Beauvoir offers us Armand as an example of ethical action in the realm of the political.

The concrete condition of political action means that all political action involves **risk**, a concept first introduced in Chapter 2 and discussed again in Chapter 7. In *The Ethics of Ambiguity*, Beauvoir makes clear that any course of action undertaken entails the possibility of moral failure and is laden with ambiguity. The use of violence, for instance, may be needed to end a history of oppression, but violence, for Beauvoir, is never unambiguously justifiable. Yet, neither the possibility of failure nor the ambiguity of action is reason for political disengagement. In fact, for Beauvoir, that we cannot rely on ideals intensifies the responsibility we each have in relation to political action. Insofar as what happens in the world, and what happens with realities of harm and oppression, is on us, we must act. An apolitical orientation would be in bad faith, allowing an individual to absolve themself of responsibility.

Just as much as Beauvoir was interested in a theory of political action, she was also just as concerned with conditions that undermine the possibility of it. In *Ethics of Ambiguity*, *America Day by Day*, and *The Second Sex* she thematizes how the existential and material conditions of oppression preempt political resistance. Although she does not go so far as to say that oppression makes resistance impossible, she is clear that certain situations conspire against it. For instance, divesting a group of individuals from formal political activity, like voting, is one way to maintain an oppressive situation, while social norms and ideals are another. She describes an instance of the latter in *America Day by Day* as she recounts her experience visiting Oberlin College, a private liberal arts college in Ohio attended mostly by white, affluent students. Beauvoir is astonished at how apolitical the students are. Many of the students just want to talk about sports or college organizations, even though they are aware of political matters and issues. Beauvoir writes,

> What is most striking to me, and most discouraging, is that they are so apathetic while being neither blind nor unconscious. They know and deplore the oppression of thirteen million blacks, the terrible poverty of the South, the almost equally desperate poverty that pollutes big cities...They know that their country is responsible for the world's future. But they themselves don't feel responsible for anything, because they don't think they can do anything in the world.
>
> ([1947] 1999, 94)

Beauvoir understands their apathy to be a result of American individualism, which, she claims, "stifles the awakening of a collective spirit" in an individual and robs one "of any concrete power" (94).

Moreover, in her consideration of myths in *The Second Sex*, Beauvoir describes at length how dominant norms and attitudes about sexual difference, as well as how the fulfillment of gendered conventions of love, sex, and desire render individuals complicit with oppression. Some of the most disconcerting descriptions of complicity with patriarchal oppression can be found in "The Girl" and "Sexual Initiation" chapters where she accounts for how girls are trained into feminine charms, into becoming desirable objects for men, to realize their own self-mutilation. "The girl—unless she is particularly graceless—accepts her femininity in the end; she is often happy to enjoy gratuitously the pleasures and triumphs she gets from settling definitively into her destiny," Beauvoir asserts ([1949] 2010, 379). Here, Beauvoir is not blaming the girl for assuming her femininity. Rather, she highlights the reality that conditions of oppression are often sources of pleasure, desire, and happiness. As a result, individuals can be complicit in their own oppression and therefore refuse and fail to see the need for political action. Her analysis in *The Second Sex* makes it crystal clear that because we are taught and encouraged to desire and participate in upholding the status quo of oppression, social and political change is not a given. It is, rather, a project we must undertake repeatedly.

Beauvoir does not see ethical political action as impossible, but she does understand it to be difficult to undertake. We can be swept away by the forces of history. We can be swept away in customs that discourage resistance to the status quo. We can be overwhelmed by material conditions that render political activity nearly impossible. We can be entrenched in social and economic conditions that obscure the realities of oppression in the first place. For these reasons, Beauvoir understands the realization of moral freedom to be difficult to achieve. And yet, even despite it all, she continues to insist on the need for solidarity and the possibility of social and political change.

MYTHS AND MYSTIFICATION

Beauvoir does not understand conditions of injustice or the reality of subordination and exploitation to be only passively experienced or the mere product of affairs and institutions external to individual experience. Even as she acknowledges that social structures and institutions shape everyone's possibilities and capacities for agency in advance of our own willing, she does not refuse the fact that our wills often give us over to perpetuating injustice. For Beauvoir, individuals abet these dire realities, consciously and unconsciously. She writes at length about how individuals positioned as sovereign subjects pursue the subordination of others as a condition of their own subjectivity. She describes how those set up to be **the Other,** that quasi-subject position in which an individual is relegated to an object status relative to a subject, are encouraged to partake, often with pleasure, in their own oppression. In other words, for Beauvoir there are no pure victims and no such thing as absolute ignorance. We are all accomplices. The question, however, for Beauvoir is: How is this the case? Or, what preempts us from pursuing social and political change? Her answer can be found in her investigation of the phenomenon of mystification.

Beauvoir's conception of mystification draws on Marxist insights about the obfuscation of oppressive and exploitative social dynamics. She considers **mystification** to be a phenomenon related to the naturalization of such dynamics and as central to individual acceptance of and participation in relations of domination and subordination. Regarding the latter, she conceives of mystification phenomenologically, paying attention to how individuals embody and experience norms and modes of relationality that perpetuate oppression as a given and even as a source of comfort and happiness. Beauvoir does not think mystification creates an unambiguous reality wherein people are fully aware or unaware of their situation, but rather she draws attention to the ideological and material economies that encourage complicity. In other words, mystification does not make us pure victims of deception; it's that social, historical, and material forces work in ways to keep us beholden to and thus incapable of perceiving realities of injustice. One of Beauvoir's central claims in *The Second Sex* is that women participate in and accept their own bondage because it is more comfortable to fall in line with the status quo than to struggle for one's freedom. "[W]ithout a doubt it is more comfortable to endure blind bondage than to work for one's liberation," she asserts, not because women are unambiguously duped by their situation but because perceiving one's reality for what it is puts moral and political demands on an individual ([1949] 2010, 274). Mystification encourages us to flee our responsibility to freedom and live in bad faith.

In her work, she examines mystification in relation to the operation of myths. **Myths**, a constellation of dominant values, ideas, narratives, and conventions about who and what we are and how the world works, shape the relationships we have with others and ourselves, as well as how we encounter and perceive the workings of the world. For Beauvoir, the circulation and embodiment of myths keep oppression and exploitation alive. As discussed in Chapters 4 and 5, her analysis of the myth of the eternal feminine in *The Second Sex* exemplifies this point. As introduced in Chapter 4, the **myth of the eternal feminine** is a collection of myths that aim to produce an image of Woman, a static ideal that obscures the diverse reality of individual women. "In concrete reality, women manifest themselves in many different ways," Beauvoir writes, "but each of the myths built around woman tries to summarize her as a whole" ([1949] 2010, 266). Central to the myths about women is the ideal of the Eternal Feminine, which characterizes the ideal woman, or Woman, as mysterious, angelic, nurturing, chaste, charming, and simultaneously, dangerous, evil, whorish, and suspicious. The circulation of the myth obscures the reality of who women really are. Or, as Beauvoir puts it, "the myth of Woman substitutes for an authentic relation with an autonomous existence the immobile contemplation of a mirage" (272). Insofar as the myth penetrates their existence, women are ensnared in it such that it also prevents them from assuming themselves as autonomous individuals.

For Beauvoir, the circulation of myths in each milieu and their pre-reflective uptake in lived experience is a central way dominant values and meanings are secured. As a result, myths are also the way concrete realities of domination and subordination are obscured in everyday experience. It is through myths, Beauvoir claims, that we escape reality through an imagistic sense of it. Rather than engage the concrete as it is, our perception of the world relies on ideals and idols.

As discussed in Chapter 4, Beauvoir accounts for the reality of American racism in *America Day by Day*, she describes how biological essentialism operates mythically to distort, or mystify, the reality of Black inferiority. "The surest way to succeed [in maintaining the status quo] is to convince oneself that the inequality between blacks and whites is not created by human will but merely confirms a given fact," Beauvoir writes ([1947] 1999, 238). The continued circulation and uptake of the myth as "fact" mystifies that Black inferiority is a reality created by white people. Ultimately, the process is justificatory. People come to accept how reality is because it is justified by the myths through which they know the world. The myth justifies the reality of inferiority even though that reality is created through the myth itself.

In various texts, including *America Day by Day*, *The Second Sex*, and *The Coming of Age*, Beauvoir draws attention to how myths govern the lives of those in power and those in positions of inferiority. Her diaries also account for the existential hold of myths on experience. In *Memoirs of a Dutiful Daughter*, for instance, Beauvoir narrates her best friend Zaza's struggle with the "formalism which governs the lives of most of the people in 'our class'" in relation to love ([1958] 1959, 322). Beauvoir also discusses how the Roman Catholic ideals she was raised with atrophied her own sexual life. "I frankly detested the Roman Catholic religion," Beauvoir writes. "I was still contaminated by it; the sexual taboos still haunted me ..." (327). Beauvoir further writes about the existential grip of these ideals in *Diary of a Philosophy Student: Volume 3, 1926–1930* where she describes her struggles with "little monsters," the internalized bourgeois, Catholic idealization of love, in the face of the beginning of her non-monogamous relationship with Sartre (2024, 181). While Beauvoir's and Zaza's personal experiences with myths of love may seem trivial to realities of domination and oppression, myths and mystification take hold of us in the intimate and everyday aspects of our lives. Not only is such experience inflected by the content of myths, but myths constitute experience through a distortion of reality. The result is that we become alienated from the concreteness of our situation and instead engage in the world through ideals and norms that mire us in abstraction. In her consideration of old age in *The Coming of Age*, Beauvoir considers how myths operate historically and culturally to confer meaning to the lived experience of age. In some contexts, myths of old age provide the aged with a high standing, while in others, myths demote the aged. Some myths associate old age with wisdom, others with folly. In each case the consequence is the same, the actual lived experience of age is covered over by myth.

In *The Second Sex*, Beauvoir describes myths of love in the "Woman in Love" chapter in which she argues that women and men have distorted experiences of love, experiences that produce and animate patriarchal oppression, because of their attachments to and investments in a variation of the myth of the eternal feminine, "the woman in love." What happens to men and women who love through the myth and thus abandon themselves in idolization? For a woman who becomes "the woman in love," the consequences of such self-abandonment are dire. "One of the misfortunes of the woman in love," Beauvoir says, "is that her love itself disfigures her, demolishes her … she is only love, and when love is deprived of its object, she is nothing" ([1949] 2010, 704). The experience of love through the myth mystifies a woman's reality. This mystification maintains and codifies patriarchal oppression insofar as the woman believes she is committed to true love when she has committed herself to love conditioned by patriarchal ideology.

The consideration of myths in *The Second Sex* offers the most robust account of our complicity with oppression. Her account of patriarchal oppression underscores how women are trained to be and take up the myth of the eternal feminine because assuming it, living out one's existence through it, affords recognition and approval. In other words, in a patriarchal world, becoming the myth, embodying the ideals of the myth are a condition of being accepted and desired. Women, then, internalize and live out patriarchal myths, and the values that underlie them, not just because others have coerced them to, but because women make a constrained choice to do so. Far from victim-blaming, however, Beauvoir's point is more that oppression is not constituted passively; it is not just scripted onto people from the outside but is taken up from within. This internal constitution of oppression mystifies the external world and the relational dynamics that produce it.

What Beauvoir uncovers about mystification and the presence of myths in our lives is that they draw us into bad faith. As discussed in Chapter 3, **bad faith** is an existential attitude or mode of assuming oneself in the world, of relating to the world, in which an individual refuses an engagement with their situation by fleeing ambiguity. In relation to the mystification of oppression, this means relying on and embodying myths that justify and perpetuate its existence. This manifestation of bad faith is not so much about being ignorant of how the world is, but of developing a distorted consciousness about the world and one's existence in it because of refusing to subject dominant ideas, values, and conventions to critical scrutiny. It is, instead, an adoption of an attitude that just assumes and therefore accepts that things just are the way they are. The consequence is that the conditions through which oppression materializes are simultaneously obscured and justified, and this reality prevents individuals from engaging in political struggle. Instead, they become actively and passively engaged with the perpetuation of oppression, which undercuts the possibility for the political labor and ideological and personal sacrifices required by liberatory struggle.

CHOOSING SOLIDARITY

When Beauvoir embarked on a six-week visit to China in September and October of 1955, she was eager to see the promises of the Communist revolution. She had, since her youth, despised the bourgeois values of capitalism, which she understood to distort the egalitarian project of democracy. Beauvoir was eager to see different political and economic structures realized for the sake of emancipatory change. She was thus interested in alternatives to bourgeois capitalism and therefore considered the possibilities of communist China. She describes the possibilities and limitations of communist China in *The Long March*, which was published in 1957, just two years after her visit. The book was an outrage to anti-Communists in America and right-wing politicians in France, for in the book, she refuses to dismiss Communism outright. Instead, Beauvoir commits to descriptions of her observations about the new political economy and the conditions of possibility for social change.

Beauvoir was deeply unsatisfied with and embarrassed by the book. She admitted it was outdated within years of its publication and believed it to be lacking in philosophical rigor. There are also inaccuracies and questionable representations in her account. But the work itself represents Beauvoir's interest in and commitment to social and political change rooted in radical structural overhauls. She did not believe in liberal or assimilationist approaches to change. She believed in struggling for political possibilities beyond reformism. As she says at the end of *The Long March*, "China is not a paradise. Obviously ... But ... this new China embodies a particularly exciting moment in history: that in which man, long reduced to dreaming of what humanity might be, is setting out to become it" ([1957] 1958, 501).

What is revealing about Beauvoir's interest in China is not her misdiagnosis of its political promise, but rather her belief that anti-capitalist, anti-bourgeois political struggle is necessary for liberation. Coupled with her feminist and anti-colonial politics, her opposition to and feelings of complicity with the violence of World War II, as well as her support of various international struggles against oppressive regimes, which is described in Chapter 7, this conception of struggle prioritizes the creation of social, material, and political conditions free of exploitation, domination, and subordination. On her account, the way to such a world, a world where social and political change is realized, is the pursuit of solidarity.

Beauvoir conceives of **solidarity** as a political phenomenon. In "Pyrrhus and Cineas," she makes clear that solidarity is not a given, but an undertaking, writing, "Initially ... freedoms are neither unified nor opposed but separated, so solidarities are created ..." ([1944] 2004, 108: 48–49). As a creation, solidarity is forged when individuals who live in the world as distinct singularities and thus as separated, *choose* to come together. This choosing is not a given. Insofar as individuals are all free to pursue their own unique projects, they are not often unified, but distinct, distant, and sometimes in conflict with one another. She does not, then, conceive of solidarity as a harmonious joining together of individuals. It is rather the activity of political struggle that bonds people together through a collective pursuit of freedom.

As discussed in Chapter 3, Beauvoir argues that authentic freedom, or moral freedom, is not purely an individual endeavor. It is true, Beauvoir says, that we can pursue our projects individualistically, that we can pursue our own desires and goals for ourselves, but that is not freedom in the moral sense. Rather, if an individual is to be free, if they are to will themself free, they must also desire and will every other individual to be. She puts this most clearly in *The Ethics of Ambiguity*, writing, "To will oneself free is to also to will others free" ([1947] 1976, 73). The realization of moral freedom therefore requires that individuals develop their own freedom by securing and promoting the freedom of others. If any condition of oppression exists it is therefore necessary, for the sake of everyone to be free, not just in theory but in the very lived, concrete, visceral way, to choose to struggle together for freedom and against oppression. Political solidarity is thus a crucial component of Beauvoir's existentialist ethics.

Beauvoir knew very well that many people do not promote the freedom of others. Her preoccupations with the tragedy of and complicity in World War II, with realities of oppression, with colonialism and capitalism, with the constraints of bourgeois ideals, and with intersubjective conflict, underscore how freedom is compromised by others. But that others do intervene and compromise freedom for all, raises the question: Why must I affirm the freedom of others? For Beauvoir, the answer rests in the reality of freedom. As she puts it in "Pyrrhus and Cineas":

> I want the other to recognize my acts as valuable, to turn them to further good by taking them up toward the future, but I cannot count on such a recognition if at the start I set myself in opposition to the other's project: he will only see an obstacle in me ... Respect for the freedom of the other is not an abstract rule: it is the first condition of my own effort.
>
> ([1944] 2004, 357–258)

In other words, for an individual's willing to be that which realizes their own existence as freedom, they must also recognize and affirm the freedom of others. This reciprocity is the condition for their respect of my freedom and thus my willing. For her, the choice we must make in the face of conditions and individuals that compromise the freedom of others is to affirm a struggle against oppression. In other words, the choice of solidarity is to choose freedom that works against the inauthentic or bad faith freedom of the oppressor; it is to choose freedom for myself that recognizes the freedom of those who resist oppression. Solidarity is the political struggle for freedom and as such, it is necessary to undertake. Beauvoir's commitments later in her life to Algerian Independence and anti-colonialism make this point clear. Through her writings, she exposed the hypocrisy of the French government to incite support for Algerian rebels amongst French citizens like herself. She publicly avowed the violent tactics of the National Liberation Front (FLN), while condemning the violence and torture used by the French government.

Beauvoir knew that solidarity is often lived in bad faith, and in her work, she is especially critical of how patriarchy undermines women's capacity to choose solidarity with and for other women. In the "Introduction" to *The Second Sex*, for instance, she notes how bourgeois women "are in solidarity with bourgeois men and not with women proletarians; as white women, they are in solidarity with white men and not with black women" ([1949] 2010, 8). By solidarity here, Beauvoir means choosing to recognize the projects of men from a shared social status over those of women from different social statuses. Such solidarity is not the kind of political solidarity that Beauvoir takes to be necessary for justice. Rather, this paradoxical, isolating solidarity speaks to how we are affected by the historical and sociopolitical conditions that underlie and structure our existence. We can feel solidarity with those who are unjust or who commit evil, a point she also makes in an "Eye for an "Eye," a political essay on justice and revenge ([1946] 2004). But this feeling is not solidarity in the political sense. It is a matter of who we feel allegiance or a connection to. That women choose men like them, for instance, is a reality of the constraints and orientations our concrete situation compels us to take up. She thus understands the absence of solidarity among women to be a result of the conditions and structures of patriarchal oppression, which works to render ethical solidarity practically impossible. Her view is that in the absence of women choosing freedom for themselves and for other women, that is, in choosing solidarity that works against oppression, patriarchy will persist.

Beauvoir's conception of transformative political solidarity is not an identity-based solidarity in a strict sense. She does not think women must *only* be in solidarity with women for patriarchal oppression to end. Rather, she thinks we all must choose solidarity that works against conditions of oppression and injustice. This political relation is a matter of choosing to form an ethical bond with those struggling against the forces that foreclose freedom and working to secure freedom concrete and materially for all. Such choosing does not, however, come easy. Given the force of history, the power of tradition and conventions, and the isolation and exploitation produced in oppressive conditions, Beauvoir does not understand political solidarity to be an overnight achievement. She does not take the realization of moral freedom to be simple or easy, or necessarily peaceful. For her, solidarity is a matter of sacrificing the status quo, of giving up social and material investments in it, and taking the risk to form bonds across oppressor and oppressed lines. In effect, solidarity is an intentional activity, an active struggle with others.

Central to Beauvoir's conception of solidarity is her notion of **reciprocity**. As discussed in Chapter 3, Beauvoir understands reciprocity to be a mode of recognition in which another individual, or a group of individuals, are affirmed in their difference but not trapped in it. Or, as Chapter 3 states, reciprocity is the recognition of the similarity and difference between self and other. This kind of recognition does not subsume another individual as like me or for me, nor does it hold another individual captive to being different from me. In the positive sense, reciprocity is the acknowledgment that the other is a freedom, which means that the material conditions and possibilities for their life and their projects must be secured. In other words, if solidarity is the political act of choosing to create genuine freedom for all, in the concrete sense, then reciprocity is the ethical relation necessary for that pursuit. Or, as Beauvoir puts it in an "Eye for an Eye": "The affirmation of the reciprocity of interhuman relations is the metaphysical basis of the idea of justice" (2004, 249).

BECOMING FREE

Beauvoir knew that freedom could be exploited. She knew that the project, the willing, of an individual or of a group could become tyrannical, that it could seek to establish itself as sovereign. In such cases, freedom is a matter of exercising power over others, rather than a lived relation of reciprocity. For Beauvoir, in situations in which there is a tyranny of a freedom, it is a perverse freedom; it is a freedom that compromises the self-other bond. In her philosophical and political writings, Beauvoir wrote about the various historical events and social circumstances in which freedom becomes perverse and through which individuals must struggle against such perversion, against domination and exploitation, to affirm reciprocity, and in turn affirm the self-other bond.

For Beauvoir, the struggle to share power *with* others, to be free with others rather than to assert freedom over and against others, is not a mere act of recognizing difference or of assimilating historically excluded groups into mainstream institutions and practices. Neither a politics of recognition nor a reformist politics create the political conditions for moral freedom. What is needed, Beauvoir argues, is concrete, material change. It is one thing, for instance, to grant women the right to vote. It is another, however, to sacrifice the family structures, conventions of intimacy, and economic relations that materially and existentially impoverish women. It is one thing, for instance, to acknowledge the history and reality of colonial violence. It is another, however, to actively work against it and support liberation, even if it means sacrificing one's comforts and privilege. What matters is that concrete, material change is pursued. And more specifically, Beauvoir insists that oppressed individuals gain the material means needed for freedom. Beauvoir speaks directly to this point in her interview with Alice Schwarzer on women's liberation. "Work is not a panacea, but all the same," Beauvoir says, "it is the first condition for independence" (Schwarzer 1984, 43). Alongside economic independence, Beauvoir insists on ending capitalism and changing sexual and social mores as necessary material conditions for freedom. Far from just an existential account of freedom, Beauvoir's politics of freedom speak to the need to redress the maldistribution of resources and to establish new, non-oppressive forms of relationality.

Beauvoir's conception of political emancipation requires social, moral, material, and political overhaul. Such political change cannot be undertaken individually. "Liberation on an individual level is not enough," Beauvoir asserts (1984, 44). "There must be collective struggle" (44). As the next chapter shows, Beauvoir participated in collective struggle for liberation throughout her life, especially in her later years. Her efforts were not perfect, but her shortcomings speak to what she knew to be true about the realization of social and political change: it's difficult work, full of complexity, contradiction, tension, and the possibility of failure. Such a reality does not, however, mean we should shy away from it. Rather, for her, living freedom requires risk, including the risk that we don't always get it right. But that risk is better than the alternative of allowing or supporting oppressive and exploitative conditions to remain.

SUGGESTED READING

Primary Texts

Beauvoir, Simone de. [1957] 1958. *The Long March*. Translated by Austryn Wainhouse. Cleveland: World Publishing.

——— [1962] 2012. "Preface to Djamila Boupacha." In *Simone de Beauvoir: Political Writings*, translated by Marybeth Timmerman, edited by Margaret A. Simons and Marybeth Timmerman, 272–282. Urbana: University of Illinois Press.

——— [1990] 2009. *Wartime Diary*. Translated by Anne Deing Cordero, edited by Sylvie Le Bon de Beauvoir, and Margaret A. Simons. Urbana: University of Illinois Press.

———— 2004. *Simone de Beauvoir: Philosophical Writings*, edited by Margaret A. Simons. Urbana: University of Illinois Press

———— 2012. *Simone de Beauvoir: Political Writings*, edited by Margaret A. Simons and Marybeth Timmerman. Urbana: University of Illinois Press.

Secondary Texts

Hutchings, Kimberly. 2007. "Simone de Beauvoir and the Ambiguous Ethics of Political Violence." *Hypatia*, 22(3): 111–132.

Kruks, Sonia. 2012. *Simone de Beauvoir and the Politics of Ambiguity*. Oxford: Oxford University Press.

Marso, Lori Jo. 2017. *Politics with Beauvoir: Freedom in the Encounter*. Durham: Duke University Press.

Schwarzer, Alice. 1984. *After "The Second Sex": Conversations with Simone de Beauvoir*. New York: Pantheon Books.

Stone, Bob, 1987. "Simone de Beauvoir and the Existential Basis of Socialism." *Social Text*, 17: 123–133.

Surkis, Judith, 2010. "Ethics and Violence: Simone de Beauvoir, Djamila Boupacha and the Algerian War." *French Politics, Culture & Society*, 28(2): 38–55.

7

WHAT MAKES LIFE MEANINGFUL?

In her autobiography, *Force of Circumstance*, Beauvoir concludes with a consideration of the kind of life she lived because of becoming, along with Sartre, "public persons" (1992b, 373). Being a public person is a reality that not only led her to protect her private life, but also subjected her to criticism from the Right and the Left about who she was, how she lived, and what she stood for. Beauvoir's response to such criticism is instructive with regard to her politics: "The only solution is to follow your own conscience and let them say what they will" (374). This response is far from cavalier, however. "Which doesn't mean that I accept my situation with a light heart," Beauvoir continues.

> The uneasiness it caused me around 1946 still persists. I know that I am a profiteer, and that I am one primarily because of the education I received and the possibilities it opened for me. I exploit no one directly; but the people who buy my books are all beneficiaries of an economy founded upon exploitation. I am an accomplice of the privileged classes and compromised by this connection.
>
> (374)

What is striking about Beauvoir's account of her status as a public person is her politicization of it. She does not take her achievements or success to be beyond the political; she takes it to be framed, structured, and inflected by it. In *All Said and Done*, the final volume of her autobiography, she echoes this

DOI: 10.4324/9781003399995-7

point, writing, "From the very beginning my birth set me up as a socially-privileged child and guaranteed me a great deal more in the way of opportunity than the daughter of a peasant or a working-class family" ([1972] 1993, 3). Perhaps even more important is that Beauvoir implicates herself in the injustice of capitalism's economic exploitation. Although written several years before the most politically active time of her life, these reflections on her privilege and political involvement, including her complicity and profiteering, highlight a political thread that can be traced, even if at times more marginally, across much of her work and life. Beauvoir had a long personal history of disdain for bourgeois values and conventions, she participated in and loathed and challenged Catholic, patriarchal ideology, she struggled with the complicity of French citizens during World War II, including her own, while also participating in resistance efforts, and, as several chapters in this book have discussed, she became invested in making visible the injustice of various forms of oppression.

It is true, even from Beauvoir's own perspective, that she became more politically involved as she got older. How Beauvoir came to assume herself in the world, how she came to be a public person in the first place, is deeply rooted in this political character. She did not become a public person because she was simply a great novelist or philosopher. She became a public person because she wrote about the world and challenged people to engage in it. In her writing she chose not to purify the world of its horrors, but to dive into them, to reveal them. For her, "[w]hen one lives in an unjust world there is no use hoping by some means to purify oneself of that injustice" (1992b, 374).

Beauvoir did not have a savior complex, however. She knew that changing the whole world was not an individual endeavor. As Chapter 6 explains, she knew the necessity of collective change. She also knew that material conditions, of both affluence and destitution, compromised people's capacity to resist injustice and pursue freedom. At the same time, in her work and life she commits to enacting her existentialist ethics of freedom. Beauvoir not only wrote about her ethical and political commitments, but she also lived them, and thus refused to do philosophy in the abstract. Indeed, her engagement with public concerns and political affairs is deeply entangled with her philosophical commitments and her practice of philosophy itself. As this chapter shows, Beauvoir's life and her philosophical legacy should also be understood as a political one, not just in terms of the content of her work, but in terms of her feminist, anti-colonial, anti-capitalist activism as a public intellectual.

POLITICAL ENGAGEMENT

In the earlier years of her teaching career, when she still clung to a kind of radical freedom abstracted from the weight of reality and had a sense of self not bound by circumstance, Beauvoir was nevertheless teaching about political matters. In *The Prime of Life*, she describes this fact with great enthusiasm. "On such subjects as labor, capital, justice, and colonialism," Beauvoir writes, "I said what I thought, and said it passionately" ([1960] 1962, 80). When her students rebelled against her claims and instead spewed out their father's bourgeois stances, Beauvoir "proceeded to demolish" them, inspiring in some of her students a "stony hatred" (80). And yet still, Beauvoir described herself as apolitical up until the 1930s. It was when Hitler's Nazi regime began to concretize and the conditions for the emergence of World War II took root, that her political engagement really solidified. "[T]here is no doubt that the spring of 1939 marked a watershed in my life," Beauvoir writes in *The Prime of Life* (285). "I renounced my individualistic, antihumanist way of life. I learned the value of solidarity" (ibid).

Beauvoir's concern with political action is evidenced in some of her earliest writings. *The Blood of Others*, which was written between 1941 and 1943 and published in 1945, is a novel about political resistance, resignation, and violence. Further, Beauvoir's consideration of responsibility in the novel underscores that moral obligation is always also a political phenomenon. For her, an individual's responsibility, as well as their experience of freedom, is shaped and constrained by the material conditions of their situation. Further, she acknowledges that what responsibility looks like is contingent on a given political context. This entanglement of ethics and political action, one that concerned Beauvoir throughout her life, is also present in "Pyrrhus and Cineas." Following these writings, Beauvoir published "Moral Idealism and Political Realism" in the November 1945 issue of *Les Temps Modernes*. In this article, Beauvoir offers one of her most explicit philosophical accounts of political action. In it, Beauvoir rejects the moralist position that "enjoins men to submit their behavior to universal, timeless imperatives, to model their actions on creation of idols inscribed in an intelligible heaven—Justice, Law, and Truth" ([1945] 2004, 177). For her, action that emerges from universal principles is removed from the concrete reality of the world. Such abstraction not only obscures political problems, but also allows individuals to flee responsibility. "Such an ethics," one rooted in eternal principles, "can be of no real help to the political man," Beauvoir asserts (177). Instead, Beauvoir insists on political action that is rooted in and emergent from the concreteness of a situation. Whereas individuals can find respite in universal imperatives when things do not turn out as desired, concrete political action, which Beauvoir takes to be ethical political action, demands individual responsibility. When politics is pursued in this way, "the political man cannot avoid questioning himself about the justification for his actions" (189). In effect, for Beauvoir, ethical political action is always laced with ambiguity for there are no guarantees, no certain outcomes, and once action is taken there is no one to blame but yourself if things go awry. This uncertainty, this risk, is the price of freedom, and Beauvoir believes it is our responsibility to embrace it.

Although one of Beauvoir's shorter and earlier essays, "Moral Idealism and Political Realism" underscores Beauvoir's commitment to neither pure idealist or pure realist positions, but to an existential ethics and politics that demands we have our feet on the ground and engage in the world as it is. As Sonia Kruks points out, it is "very much a text for its times" (Kruks 2004, 168).

> Beauvoir's inquiry is driven by her passionate concern about concrete political events and actions: the loss of life that had resulted from the French Resistance; the claims of Nazi

collaborators (then on trial) to have acted for "principled" ends, such as saving France from further bloodshed; and the question of means and ends as it was unfolding above all in the trajectory of the Russian Revolution.

(ibid)

Even, then, in her less overt times as an activist, this passionate concern is central to her work. Indeed, the horrors of World War II, especially the extent of individual's complicity with evil and Beauvoir's own reckoning with what concrete resistance should look like, fueled a good deal of her writing. But, as is apparent in "Right Wing Thought Today," published in 1955, in which she critiques the bourgeois ideologies of right-wing politics, Beauvoir's commitment to the concrete and to the ambiguity of political action does not always come forth in her writing. In that piece in particular, Beauvoir's writing is abstract and her challenge to the ideology of the bourgeois ruling class is dichotomous. She insists that to be against the privileged means one must be with the Communists of the time.

Such polarized thinking is precisely one that the journal that published the piece, *Les Temps Modernes*, sought to undermine. In 1945, in the immediate aftermath of the war, Beauvoir co-founded the radical, Leftist journal, *Les Temps Modernes*, along with Sartre and Merleau-Ponty. The intent of the journal was to influence society, and Beauvoir, like Sartre, Merleau-Ponty and other contributing writers, wrote for *Les Temps Modernes* as an appeal for political engagement and as a venue to expose and critique injustice. More specifically, they wanted to create an intellectual platform for democratic socialism, a venue critical of capitalism, bourgeois liberalism, and rigid Communism.

The journal wasn't Beauvoir's first foray into political writing for a public audience, however. She published two articles on the oppression and injustice of the working classes in Spain and Portugal in *Combat*, a French Resistance paper, edited at the time by fellow existentialist Albert Camus. Beauvoir's understanding of injustice and freedom as materially conditioned is prominent in these pieces. She writes about the prominent class divisions and the injustice of poverty that leaves many lacking in necessities. Central to these reports is a critique of capitalism's class divisions. In "Portugal Under the Salazar Regime" ([1945] 2012), Beauvoir describes a reaction she received from a rich Portuguese man after she gave money to a poor, hungry child on the street near the restaurant they were at. The rich man attempts to take the money from the child, but Beauvoir obstructs him from doing so. While "serving himself a decadent bite of foot, the rich man scolds Beauvoir: 'he [the child] will buy cigarettes and candy for himself!'" ([1945] 2012, 26). "The violence of such a reaction illustrates well the hatred that the rich over there have for the poor," Beauvoir writes about this experience (ibid). She continues, "They [the rich] fear them [the poor], for they know very well that their fortune is the fruit of a shameful exploitation" (ibid). In an article published in 1971, "In France Today, Killing Goes Unpunished," Beauvoir returns to such exploitation, exposing the injustice of poor working conditions endured by the proletariat, and in particular, the injuries sustained in a factory fire.

These initial public-facing political writings were a precursor to later, and often more direct, political appeals Beauvoir made to the public. Such appeals were especially clear when it came to Beauvoir's opposition to France's colonial violence during the Algerian revolution. Her support of and advocacy of Djamila Boupacha is one prime example of such an appeal. In 1960, at 23 years old, Boupacha, an Algerian activist for the National Liberation Front (FLN) in the fight against the colonial French Army for Algerian independence, was arrested and accused of terrorism. After refusing to confess to the charges brought against her, Boupacha was tortured and raped by the French Army. Working with Boupacha's lawyer, Gisèle Halimi, Beauvoir first authored an article in the French newspaper *Le Monde* to galvanize the French public and expose the violence and hypocrisy of the French government. The article, "In Defense of Djamila Boupacha," was published on June 3, 1960. In it, Beauvoir demands readers to confront, rather than ignore the reality of torture. Philosopher Julien S. Murphy notes how "[i]n her memoir, Beauvoir minimized the political content and impact of her *Le Monde* article … It was actually a scathing indictment of the Army … She pricked the conscience of the reader by charging every citizen in France as an accomplice to torture" (Murphy 2012, 264). As a French citizen, Beauvoir implicated herself in the torture as well, feeling burdened with responsibility for France's colonial violence. Beauvoir's condemnation was so significant the French government had all copies of the Algerian edition destroyed so as to not encourage further resistance.

In 1962, Beauvoir wrote the preface for the book *Djamila Boupacha* in which she makes clear the choice of complicity or solidarity that French people have. For Beauvoir, such a choice is not a false dichotomy. In the face of oppression, there are two choices: side with the oppressors or side with the oppressed, conspire with the oppressor or struggle against the oppressor. That is, as she writes at the end of preface, "You can either take sides with the torturers of those who are suffering today and passively consent to the martyrdom they endure in your name, almost under your noses ... or you can not only refuse certain practices, but the end that authorizes and demands them" ([1962] 2012, 281). Beauvoir's point is that, in the face of evil, the choices of any individual are clear: either support those who foreclose freedom for some or undertake the political project of solidarity. She considers the latter to be the moral choice.

Her political engagement was not limited to writing. Even prior to her more prominent role as a feminist activist, Beauvoir was politically active. Along with other French intellectuals, she signed the Manifesto of the 121 in support of Algerian independence and insubordination against the French regime, which was published on September 6, 1960. She would continue to sign petitions to speak out against unjust governments. As Deirdre Bair details in her biography of Beauvoir, "From 1970 until the mid-1980s ... Petitions she signed include those protesting the death sentence of Basque nationalists, appeals to the Soviet government for Jewish immigration to Israel, and many Latin-American protest petitions" (Bair 1990, 550). During this time, Beauvoir took it to be of the utmost importance to be public about her politics. She understood the significance of giving her name and her platform to those being persecuted and to the realities of injustice. Yet, as the final section of this chapter makes clear, this did not mean Beauvoir always got it right.

What is clear about Beauvoir's political involvement is that she was willing to assume responsibility for the world as it was and could be. Central to her existentialist ethics, as discussed in Chapter 2, are the ideas of the appeal and risk. For Beauvoir, an **appeal** is a political phenomenon; it is a matter of reaching out to and insisting that others take up your political projects and commitments. Not all appeals are ethical. They do not all seek to affirm the bond between self and others and create the material conditions that make it possible for all to be free. For Beauvoir, it is also true that some appeals are heard more than others, that circumstances can silence some appeals or make it difficult for individuals to make appeals. In many ways, this is perhaps why Beauvoir sought to use her status to give voice to injustice, to the experiences of those living in persecution, overwhelmed by violence, to those who were existentially, economically, politically, and socially robbed of the possibility to be heard in the first place. Beauvoir's appeals were, consistent with her philosophical commitments, done not just in the name of freedom, but to concretely realize freedom. There is, though, **risk** in any appeal and in freedom itself. Insofar as Beauvoir understands the values, meanings, and circumstances of the world to be a matter of human activity, what we choose, what political activity we undertake, always involves the possibility of uncertainty and so, too, of failure. Others may reject an individual's appeal or an individual's appeal may take an unexpected course, not just because of how or if others take it up, but because of the way an individual's particular situation limits how they perceive the world to be in the first place.

Whenever Beauvoir authored a political essay, there was no guarantee that her appeals would be heard or heard in the ways she had hoped. Insofar as all perspectives are situated and therefore limited by their situation, it is also the case that an individual's appeal may have shortcomings they cannot perceive. There is risk, then, in an appeal itself. When we undertake projects to realize **moral freedom**, the kind of freedom that pursues an ethical bond with others, the risk is in the fact that an individual cannot guarantee that their appeal, that their political action, is or will do what they hope. Such is the ambiguity at the heart of political action, and this reality shows up in Beauvoir's undertakings. At the same time, even if her political life was imperfect, it would be remiss to not take seriously that Beauvoir sought to live out her ideas. She was not an armchair philosopher. Her life as a philosopher, as a public person, was entangled with progressive, and often radical, political action.

FEMINIST ACTIVISM

Beauvoir's most well-known political activism, her feminist activism, did not begin until 1970 when she joined in the efforts of the *Mouvement de libération des femmes* (MLF). At 62 years old, she hosted small meetings with MLF founders and organizers, mostly young women in their 20s, in her apartment. At one of these meetings, she signed the Manifesto of the 343 ("Manifeste des 343"), a public declaration of 343 women who admitted to having an abortion at a time when it was still illegal in France. As Beauvoir writes in the final volume of her autobiography, *All Said and Done*, the MLF wanted her "to speak on the new abortion bill that was soon to come before parliament" ([1972] 1993, 444). Having already written against the repression of abortion in *The Second Sex*, Beauvoir agreed. The manifesto was published in *Le Nouvel Observateur* on April 5, 1971. The purpose was to lay bare the reality of abortion and to uncover its regularity in order to advocate for its legalization. The MLF hoped it would create a stir, and it did. "[N]aturally much of the attention was focused on Beauvoir," writes Bair (1990, 547). This attention wasn't new; she "had been the favorite target of right-wing writers and publications for years" (547). Immediately after the manifesto's publication, French media outlets were using the word 'abortion' regularly for the first time in French history and the fight for legalized abortion had officially launched.

At a time when abortion was illegal, such a declaration was a bold move. Beauvoir, along with all the women who signed the manifesto, exposed themselves to criminal prosecution, as well as social criticism. As Kate Kirkpatrick, author of the biography *Becoming Beauvoir* writes, "Unsurprisingly, the signatories were slurred as the '343 sluts'" (Kirkpatrick 2019, 347). Beauvoir claims she never had an abortion, so implicating herself in such illegal activity was a way to give social action to her words. She also knew that her privilege was protection, which she chose to wield politically. Or, in her words, "I believed that it was up to women like me to take the risk on behalf of those who could not, because we could afford to do it. We had the money and the position and we were not likely to be punished for our actions" (Bair 1990, 547). But, Beauvoir didn't just sign a manifesto. She "frequently allowed illegal abortions to be performed in her apartment when women had no other choice, and she often paid for them, whether they were carried out in her apartment or somewhere else" (Bair 1990, 547).

In many respects, "The Manifesto of the 343" was a gateway for Beauvoir's feminist activism. In July 1971, Beauvoir became the first president of the French pro-choice organization, *Choisir*, which she co-founded with four other notable feminists, Gisèle Halimi, Jean Rostand, Christiane Rochefort, and Jacques Monod. "The group had three objectives," Kirkpatrick notes (2019, 356), "[T]o educate women about sex and contraception; change the French law on abortion, which had been in place since 1920; and to provide women who had had abortions with free legal defence" (356). A few months later, on November 11, 1971, Beauvoir took to the streets of Paris to march with thousands of other women to demand the legal right to abortion. In 1972, Beauvoir spoke publicly on behalf of *Choisir* in Grenoble and attended and offered public support at the "Bobigny Trial," in which 16-year-old Marie-Claire Chevalier was on trial for having an abortion after being raped. When the fight for abortion rights was close to secure, Beauvoir co-founded and served as the first President of the League of Women's Rights, which Beauvoir saw as a platform to advocate for anti-sexist legislation. As Kirkpatrick notes, "The League met with opposition from fellow feminists, who saw it as a concession to or even collaboration with the bourgeois and patriarchal framework of the legal system" (2019, 367). But, at this point in her life, Beauvoir felt that laws against sexism could undercut how it hindered women's experience and freedom. Moreover, Beauvoir "conducted an inquiry for the leftist publication *J'accuse*, to help women injured in a factory accident at Méru in their fight for compensation. She sat in at the CET technical college, really a home where unwed mothers were shunted until their babies were born" (Bair 1990, 550).

In the early 1970s, Beauvoir also wielded her pen and access to intellectual platforms as a form of feminist activism. She created a column called "Everyday Sexism" in *Les Temps Modernes* for "those who wanted to denounce sexism," which allowed feminists of her time who did not support the League of Women's Rights' turn to legal reform to have a platform for social critique and subversive politics (Kirkpatrick 2019, 367). From here on out, Beauvoir expanded her own feminist writing, giving voice to issues and experiences marginalized by the mainstream. She wrote about marriage, divorce, abortion, and same-sex desire, among other topics, and served as the Publication Director for the radical feminist theory magazine *Questions Féministes*. This wasn't a first for Beauvoir. She had an established history of writing feminist pieces for popular venues. She published a critique of femininity in *Vogue* in 1947, wrote about patriarchy's cooptation of love in the April 1950 issue of *Flair*, a short-lived American fashion magazine, and delivered three lectures in Japan in 1966, of which the first was on women's situation in the bourgeois democracies of Japan, France, and the United States. What is consistent across these efforts is Beauvoir's commitment to engaging the public, by using her intellectual voice to appeal to the public to take up feminist concerns.

At the end of the 1970s, as the political stage shifted once again and the women's movement changed course, Beauvoir's feminist activism persisted. She became president of the International Committee for Women's Rights in 1979 as part of her involvement in the Iranian Revolution. As she detailed in her opening statement as president on March 15, 1979, the purpose of this committee "was to inform themselves and the global public of the situation of women in each country throughout the world, and to support the actions and struggles of women for their rights" (Picq 2015, 238). At the center of this objective was to support women in Iran against any pending attacks on their freedom. Consistent with her prior political activity, Beauvoir took to the international stage to denounce and expose violations of women's freedom, as well as to secure political, economic, and social conditions in which women could concretely realize their freedom.

Beauvoir's feminist activism is not only important because of the extent of her involvement in the 1970s, but also because her involvement was a realization of her philosophical and political commitments in *The Second Sex*. Her activism challenged social conventions that restricted women's freedom. Her activism exposed economic repression that enabled women's subordination and the material conditions that barred them from freedom. Her activism decried the patriarchal institution of marriage and fought for women's sexual freedom. At each turn, Beauvoir willingly used her intellectual and economic status to advance feminist causes and willingly put herself on the line when beneficial for the collective good. Beauvoir, however, stuck to her own political commitments as well, which meant she didn't always agree with every feminist activist or action. She denounced separatism and the "women's writing" movement, or *l'écriture féminine*, which emerged among a group of French feminists in the mid-1970s. She was also accused of being complicit in patriarchal conventions in her relationship with and commitment to Sartre. Yet, even as Beauvoir often acknowledged her own complicity with patriarchal conventions, "could she see all of them?" (Kirkpatrick 2019, 369). Likely not. She was not an ideal, feminist heroine, but without a doubt, in the later years of her life, she did strive to politically realize her feminist beliefs.

LIVING IN THE WORLD WITH OTHERS

Central to the animating philosophical issue of Beauvoir's legacy—the relation between the self and the other—is an interest in the entanglement of the ethical and the political. She understood how political action could undermine or secure the bond between self and others. She also acknowledged how the relation between self and others was not just a matter of ethics, but a political matter through and through. Her reflections on love, sex, and desire in her novels and in essays like "Must

We Burn Sade?" make clear that intimacy itself, those experiences generally perceived as "private" and thus separate from the political realm, are not only political, but are also the site wherein realities of domination, exploitation, and subordination take hold of us in the most powerful of ways. This phenomenological dimension of Beauvoir's political disposition is unique to her legacy. Freedom, as well as injustice, are intimate and embodied phenomena. We live them out not just in more formal or overt political activity, but in the vulnerability of our flesh, in the ways we are touched by others, and in how others intervene in our lives.

This overlap of the political with the personal is apparent in Beauvoir's life, often in vexed ways. Over the course of her life, she reckoned with the reality of her privilege and sought to use it politically, even if not always perfectly. Beauvoir's disdain for the bourgeois elite is apparent in her political efforts and her critiques of social customs and injustice. She acknowledged the extent that her childhood prepared her for the social and economic privilege she acquired. She saw the reality of racial oppression and understood its harms, but moved easily about the world through her whiteness, and, as many of her contemporary readers point out, she did not always talk about colonial and racial injustices. She grappled with her status as a woman who was subjected to patriarchal ideology and conventions and she also managed to struggle against and even escape many of them. She refused the bourgeois, Catholic conventions of love, marriage, and motherhood. She pursued her own economic and sexual freedom when it was uncommon for women to do so. She did not hide her nonmonogamy from the public. She also did not hide that she had sexual relationships with women during a time when bisexuality and lesbianism were still stigmatized.

But, this aspect of Beauvoir's life is not without complications. Her commitment to Sartre, which, in *All Said and Done* she describes as the "one undoubted success in my life," was often scrutinized by others as antithetical to her feminism ([1972] 1993, 365). As Beauvoir herself notes, "This relationship has been stigmatized by some as a contradiction of the view on morality expressed in *The Second Sex*: I insist that women be independent, yet I have never been alone" (365– 366). At the same time, Beauvoir did not relinquish herself to Sartre. She had a life and love without him, even as their bond was unwavering. As discussed in Chapter 1, in relationships where her actions were more questionable, especially in her relationships with Olga Kosakiewicz and Bianca Bienenfield, Beauvoir's own ethics are called into question. Her deception with these women highlights what Beauvoir knew to be true: ethical bonds do not come easily. In no way does this mean ethical bonds are impossible or that Beauvoir's behavior is excusable. Rather, it shows that, in the thick of the world, in the thick of one's life, in the thick of love even, it is very possible to make decisions that fail the self-other bond. Insofar as that failure undermines freedom, according to Beauvoir's own commitments, it is both a moral and political failure.

Beauvoir did not excuse herself from such failures. In an interview with Alice Schwarzer, Beauvoir makes clear that others suffered because of how she and Sartre conducted their relationship. "[O]ur relationship is not above criticism, any more than anyone else's" Beauvoir says. "[I]t has sometimes meant that we didn't behave very well towards people" (Schwarzer 1984, 53). When Schwarzer asks Beauvoir, "So other people have suffered?" Beauvoir replies straightforwardly, "Yes, exactly" (53). Beauvoir also had to come to terms with her own wrongdoing in relation to having signed the Vichy Oath, declaring she wasn't Jewish. Such a declaration made her in some way complicit with France's puppet government of Hitler's Nazi regime. Initially, Beauvoir did not consider refusing to sign as having any political significance. She did it to keep her job, to have an income during wartime, and thought, because she was a nobody at the time, that her refusal would be meaningless (Bair 1990, 242). Such a view flies in the face of her notions of risk and of solidarity, and she came to regret her choice to sign the oath.

That Beauvoir's life and her politics were not without their limits, failures, and regrets is an indication not just of the imperfections of being human, but also of the fact that living well with others isn't an idealistic pursuit. In Beauvoir we find not an idol or a perfect moral heroine, but a human being whose actions did not always realize her commitments. Her failures, just as much as her successes, are instructive. They show us how our actions can sever the self-other bond. Just as much as her political efforts do, her own shortcomings also offer insight into the importance of political action and embodying one's ethical and political commitments.

A LIFE WORTH LIVING

When Beauvoir died on April 14, 1986, she had lived a rich life, one that had inspired people around the world. Despite being sidelined for decades by the patriarchal framing of her as merely Sartre's mistress and disciple, Beauvoir was undoubtedly a philosopher, public intellectual, and political activist in her own right. For her, living is philosophical activity. It is what we do in and with our lives that matters. What her work and her life suggest to us is that a meaningful life is a life lived in the pursuit of freedom not just for oneself, but for the sake of creating ethical relations *with* others. For Beauvoir, true freedom is a relational experience undermined by realities of injustice. For her, it is necessary to live a life that challenges them, that tends to the experiences of those who are overwhelmed, existentially and materially, by the weight of injustice. Beauvoir's life and her work make clear that living a life to end the suffering of others is what makes life meaningful.

SUGGESTED READING

Primary Texts

Beauvoir, Simone de. 2012. *Simone de Beauvoir: Political Writings*, edited by Margaret A. Simons and Marybeth Timmerman. Urbana: University of Illinois Press.

———— 2015. *Feminist Writings*. Edited by M.A. Simons and M.B. Timmerman. Urbana: University of Illinois Press.

Secondary Texts

Bair, Deidre. 1990. *Simone de Beauvoir: A Biography*. New York: Summit Books.
Altman, Meryl. 2020. *Beauvoir in Time*. Leiden, The Netherlands: Brill.

Cleary, Skye. 2022. *How to be Authentic: Simone de Beauvoir and the Quest for Fulfillment*, New York: St. Martin's Essentials.

Kirkpatrick, Kate, 2019. *Becoming Beauvoir: A Life*. London: Bloomsbury.

Murphy, Julien S. 2012. "Introduction." In *Simone de Beauvoir: Political Writings*, edited by Margaret A. Simons and Marybeth Timmerman, 261–271. Urbana: University of Illinois Press.

Picq, Francoise. 2015. "Introduction." *Simone de Beauvoir: Feminist Writings*, edited by Margaret A. Simons and Marybeth Timmerman, 231–239. Urbana: University of Illinois Press.

GLOSSARY

Ambiguity Refers to the ontological condition of being human, namely that human existence is always both internality and externality, mind and matter, subject and object.

Appeal The activity of calling on others to take up and affirm one's project, including the values that underpin it.

Authenticity For Beauvoir, this notion refers to a particular way of relating to ourselves, others, and the world through which we realize freedom.

Bad faith A wide range of existential attitudes, or a disposition or way of assuming one's existence in the world, that allow us to flee from freedom and, in turn, allows us to flee responsibility for ourselves, others, and the world.

Becoming This notion refers to the reality of a thing or existence as indeterminate, historically bound, and contingent.

Being A philosophical concept that refers to an internal, predetermined, and unchanging essence of a thing.

Being for-itself An embodied self-constituting consciousness with their own purposive activity.

Being for-others How an individual's existence is constructed through the perception others have of them.

Biological Essentialism The belief that physiology or biology fully determines who one is. In relation to gender, this belief means that "woman" is a biological phenomenon, meaning that who is a woman is determined by biology.

Contingent That which is bound to the particularity of circumstance.

Embodied consciousness A phenomenological conception of subjectivity that posits that to be human is to be neither pure mind nor pure matter, but always body *and* mind.

Existentialism An intellectual movement and mode of philosophical inquiry with no definitive method, but some shared commitments, most notably that there is no human essence or human nature, and that we are always in the process of creating and giving meaning to our existence.

Existential Attitude A disposition or way of assuming one's existence in the world.

Existential Choice For Beauvoir, this refers to a constrained notion of choice. For her, although humans have the capacity to choose, we are not free to choose whatever we want. What we choose, what we can choose, and the ease with which we are able to choose from an open array of possibilities, is conditioned by values, norms, meanings, and arrangements that mediate and structure our lived experience.

Facticity The factical dimension of our lives, the ones that are inevitable, such as the reality that there are others in the world or that humans, as a species, have basic needs that must be met to stay alive.

Feminine existence A constrained, patriarchal mode of subjectivity women are socialized into. Beauvoir argues this mode of gendered subjectivity is a mutilation insofar as patriarchal femininity robs women of their capacity to assume themselves as transcendence.

Feminist Phenomenology A distinct way of doing phenomenology that considers gender as a quasi-transcendental structure of experience and offers not an account of gender as a social construction, but an account of gender as it is lived and disclosed in lived experience.

Immanence Beauvoir uses this term in *The Second Sex* to describe the life-sustaining, passive, and cyclical aspects of being human, which she understands to be related to the factical dimension of human existence.

Intentionality A phenomenological concept that describes consciousness as a directedness toward an object; it is to be "conscious of" an object.

Intersubjectivity The relation and opposition between self and other(s).

Lived body This is a phenomenological concept that refers not to the physiological, biological body, but to experience as bodily and a subject's body as an experiential phenomenon.

Lived experience This is a concept in the philosophical tradition and method of phenomenology. It refers to first-person, subjective experience. For Beauvoir, first-person experience is historically, culturally, and socially situated.

Metaphysical novel A form and style that reveals the contingency of the world, along with its multiple, interwoven meanings, bringing to light contradictions of circumstance and human choices.

Moral freedom A conception of freedom that Beauvoir understands as a kind of social bond or mode of relationality in which we strive to live in ways that hold open possibilities for one another.

Mystification A phenomenon related to the naturalization and obfuscation of oppressive and exploitative social dynamics. Beauvoir takes mystification to be central to individual acceptance of and participation in relations of domination and subordination.

Myths A constellation of dominant values, ideas, narratives, and conventions about who and what we are and how the world works, which shapes the relationships we have with others and ourselves, as well as how we encounter and perceive the workings of the world.

Myth of the eternal feminine A master myth that produces an ideology of women's "natural" inferiority to justify patriarchal domination that not only structures but is also taken up in embodied experience. The myth works to ensnare women in an unattainable ideal, which undermines their existence as individuals.

Natural Attitude In phenomenology, this concept refers to the everyday, taken-for-granted experience and understanding of a given phenomenon.

Necessity The factical aspects of the world and of being human.

Ontological freedom A notion that takes freedom to be a pure, grounding condition of being human.

Phenomenology A tradition and method of philosophy, founded by German philosopher Edmund Husserl, that studies the structure of first-person experience.

Projects World-building activity and commitments we actively take up and that are constitutive and an articulation of who we each are.

Reciprocity A mode of recognition in which another individual, or a group of individuals, are affirmed in their difference but not trapped in it. Such recognition hinges on recognizing singularity and respecting distance.

Risk The inescapable uncertainty that lies at the heart of every project; it is the reality that there is no guarantee that others will affirm any project one undertakes or that their project will have the outcomes they desire.

Situation The bodily and concrete condition of individual existence. For Beauvoir, one's body is their grasp on the world, the way to have a world, but it is not determinative of who one is.

Solidarity The activity of political struggle that bonds people together through a collective pursuit of freedom.

The Other This notion names a subordinated and dominated quasi-subject position, constituted by a perverse relation between self and other.

Transcendence Beauvoir uses this term to refer to the meaning-making and world-building dimensions of our lives. She understands it as future-oriented and related to the movement of freedom.

REFERENCES

PRIMARY TEXTS

Beauvoir, Simone de. [1943]1954. *She Came to Stay*, translated by Yvonne Moyse and Roger Senhouse. Cleveland: World Publishing.

———— [1944] 2004. "Pyrrhus and Cineas." In *Simone de Beauvoir: Philosophical Writings*, translated by Marybeth Timmerman, edited by Margaret Simons, 89–149. Urbana and Chicago: University of Illinois Press.

———— [1945] 1964. *The Blood of Others*, translated by Yvonne Moyse and Roger Senhouse. New York: Penguin Books.

———— [1945] 2004. "Moral Idealism and Political Realism." *Simone de Beauvoir: Philosophical Writings*, translated by Anne Deing Cordero, edited by Margaret A. Simons, 175–193. Urbana: University of Illinois Press.

———— [1945] 2012. "Portugal Under the Salazar Regime." In *Simone de Beauvoir: Political Writings*, translated by Marybeth Timmerman, edited by Margaret A. Simons and Marybeth Timmerman, 22–28. Urbana: University of Illinois Press.

———— [1945]2011. "The Useless Mouths." In *Simone de Beauvoir: "The Useless Mouths" and Other Literary Writings*, translated by Liz Stanley and Catherine Naji, edited by Margaret Simons and Marybeth Timmerman, 9–89. Urbana and Chicago: University of Illinois Press.

———— [1946]1955. *All Men Are Mortal*, translated by Leonard M. Friedman. Cleveland: World Publishing.

———— [1946] 2004, "An Eye for an Eye." In *Simone de Beauvoir: Philosophical Writings*, translated by Kristana Arp, edited by Margaret Simons, 245–260. Urbana and Chicago: University of Illinois Press.

———— [1947] 1976. *The Ethics of Ambiguity*, translated by Bernard Frechtman. New York: Citadel Press.

———— [1947] 1999. *America Day by Day*, translated by Carol Cosman. Berkeley: University of California Press.

————1947 [2004]. "What is Existentialism?" In *Simone de Beauvoir: Philosophical Writings*, translated by Marybeth Timmerman, edited by Margaret Simons, 323–326. Urbana and Chicago: University of Illinois Press.

———— 1949. *Le Deuxième Sexe*, Paris: Editions Gallimard.

———— [1949] 1953. *The Second Sex*, translated by H.M. Parshley. New York: Alfred A. Knopf.

———— [1949] 2010. *The Second Sex*, translated by Constance Borde and Shelia Malovany-Chevallier. New York: Alfred A. Knopf.

———— [1951–52] 2012. "Must We Burn Sade?" In *Simone de Beauvoir: Political Writings*, translated Kim Allen Gleed, Marilyn Gaddis Rose, and Virginia Preston, edited by Margaret A. Simons and Marybeth Timmerman, 44–101. Urbana: University of Illinois Press.

———— [1954] 1956. *The Mandarins*, translated by Leonard M. Friedman. Cleveland: World Publishing.

———— [1955]2012. "Right Wing Thought Today." In *Simone de Beauvoir: Political Writings*, translated by Véronique Zaytzeff and Frederick M. Morrison, edited by Margaret A. Simons and Marybeth Timmerman, 113–193. Urbana: University of Illinois Press.

———— [1957] 1958. *The Long March*, translated by Austryn Wainhouse. Cleveland: World Publishing.

———— [1958] 1959. *Memoirs of a Dutiful Daughter*, translated by James Kirkup. Cleveland: World Publishing.

———— [1960] 1962. *The Prime of Life: The Autobiography of Simone de Beauvoir*, translated by Peter Green. Cleveland: World Publishing.

———— [1962] 2012. "Preface to Djamila Boupacha." In *Simone de Beauvoir: Political Writings*, edited by Margaret A. Simons and Marybeth Timmerman, 272–282. Urbana: University of Illinois Press.

———— [1963] 1992a. *The Force of Circumstance, I: The Autobiography of Simone de Beauvoir 1944–1952*, translated by Richard Howard. New York: Paragon House.

———— [1963] 1992b. *The Force of Circumstance, II: The Autobiography of Simone de Beauvoir 1952–1962*, translated by Richard Howard. New York: Paragon House.

———— [1964] 1966. *A Very Easy Death*, translated by Patrick O'Brian. New York: Putnam.

———— [1966] 1968. *Les Belles Images*, translated by Patrick O'Brian. New York: Putnam.

———— [1970] 1972. *The Coming of Age*, translated by Patrick O'Brian. New York: Putnam.

——— [1972] 1993. *All Said and Done: The Autobiography of Simone de Beauvoir 1962–1972*. Translated by Patrick O'Brian. New York: Paragon House.

——— [1979] 1982. *When Things of The Spirit Come First: Five Early Tales*, translated by Patrick O'Brian. New York: Pantheon Books.

——— [1981] 1984. *Adieux: A Farewell to Sartre*, translated by Patrick O'Brian. New York: Pantheon Books.

——— 2004. *Simone de Beauvoir: Philosophical Writings*, edited by Margaret A. Simons. Urbana: University of Illinois Press.

——— 2006. *Diary of a Philosophy Student: Volume 1, 1926–27*, translated by Barbara Klaw, edited by Sylvie Le Bon de Beauvoir, Margaret A. Simons, and Marybeth Timmerman. Urbana: University of Illinois Press.

——— [1990] 2009. *Wartime Diary*, translated by Anne Deing Cordero, edited by Sylvie Le Bon de Beauvoir, and Margaret A. Simons. Urbana: University of Illinois Press.

——— 2012. *Simone de Beauvoir: Political Writings*, edited by Margaret A. Simons and Marybeth Timmerman. Urbana: University of Illinois Press.

——— 2015. *Simone de Beauvoir: Feminist Writings*, edited by Margaret A. Simons and Marybeth Timmerman. Urbana: University of Illinois Press.

——— 2019. *Diary of a Philosophy Student: Volume 2, 1928–29*, translated by Barbara Klaw, edited by Sylvie Le Bon de Beauvoir, Margaret A. Simons, and Marybeth Timmerman. Urbana: University of Illinois Press.

——— 2024. *Diary of a Philosophy Student: Volume 3, 1926–30*, translated by Barbara Klaw, edited by Sylvie Le Bon de Beauvoir and Margaret A. Simons. Urbana: University of Illinois Press.

SECONDARY TEXTS

Ahmed, Sara. 2006. *Queer Phenomenology*. Durham and London: Duke University Press.

Altman, Meryl. 2020. *Beauvoir in Time*. Leiden, The Netherlands: Brill.

Anderson, Ellie. 2014. "The Other: Limits of Knowledge in Beauvoir's Ethics of Reciprocity." *Journal of Speculative Philosophy* 28(3): 380–388.

Arp, Kristana. 2001. *The Bonds of Freedom: Simone de Beauvoir's Existentialist Ethics*. Chicago: Open Court.

Bair, Deidre. 1990. *Simone de Beauvoir: A Biography*. New York: Summit Books.

Bauer, Nancy, 2001. *Simone de Beauvoir, Philosophy, and Feminism*. New York: Columbia University Press.

Belle, Kathryn Sophia. 2010. "Sartre, Beauvoir, and the Race/Gender Analogy: A Case for Black Feminist Philosophy." In *Convergences: Black Feminism and Continental Philosophy*, edited by Donna-Dale L. Marcano, Kathryn T. Gines (now Belle), and Maria del Guadalupe, 35–51. Albany: SUNY Press.

———— 2014. "Comparative and Competing Frameworks of Oppression in Simone de Beauvoir's The Second Sex." *Graduate Faculty Philosophy Journal*, 35(1–2): 251–273.

———— 2017. "Simone de Beauvoir and the Race/Gender Analogy in The Second Sex Revisited." In *A Companion to Simone de Beauvoir*, edited by Laura Hengehold and Nancy Bauer, 47–58. New York: Wiley.

———— 2024. *Beauvoir and Belle: A Black Feminist Critique of* The Second Sex. Oxford: Oxford University Press.

Bergoffen, Debra. 1997. *The Philosophy of Simone de Beauvoir: Gendered Phenomenologies, Erotic Generosities*. Albany, NY: State University of New York Press.

Berruz, Stephanie Rivera. 2016. "At the Crossroads: Latina Identity and Simone de Beauvoir's *The Second Sex*." *Hypatia*, 31(2): 319–333.

Butler, Judith. 1986. "Sex and Gender in Simone de Beauvoir's The Second Sex." *Yale French Studies*. 72: 35–49.

———— 1990. *Gender Trouble: Feminism and the Subversion of Identity*. New York: Routledge.

Cleary, Skye. 2022. *How to be Authentic: Simone de Beauvoir and the Quest for Fulfillment*, New York: St. Martin's Essentials.

Cohen Shabot, Sara and Yaki Menschenfreund. "Is Existentialist Authenticity Unethical? De Beauvoir on Ethics, Authenticity, and Embodiment." *Philosophy Today*, 52(2): 150–156.

Daigle, Christine and Jacob Golomb, eds. 2009. *Beauvoir and Sartre: The Riddle of Influence*, Bloomington: Indiana Univ Press.

Deutscher, Penelope. 2008. *The Philosophy of Simone de Beauvoir: Ambiguity, Conversion, Resistance*. Cambridge: Cambridge University Press.

Fallaize, Elizabeth, ed. 1998. *Simone de Beauvoir: A Critical Reader*. London: Routledge.

Fullbrook, Edward and Kate Fullbrook. 1998. *Simone de Beauvoir: A Critical Introduction*. Cambridge: Polity Press.

Garcia, Manon. [2018] 2021. *We Are Not Born Submissive: How Patriarchy Shapes Women's Lives*. Princeton: Princeton University Press.

hooks, bell. 2012. "True Philosophers: Beauvoir and bell." In *Beauvoir and Western Thought from Plato to Butler*, edited by Shannon M. Mussett and William S. Wilkerson, 227–236. Albany: SUNY Press.

Kirkpatrick, Kate, 2019. *Becoming Beauvoir: A Life*. London: Bloomsbury.

Kristeva, Julia. [1979] 1981. "Women's Time," translated by Alice Jardine and Harry Blake. *Signs* 7(11): 7–35.

Kruks, Sonia. 1990. *Situation and Human Existence: Freedom, Subjectivity and Society*, New York: Routledge.

———— 2004. "Introduction." In *Simone de Beauvoir: Philosophical Writings*, edited by Margaret A. Simons, 167–173. Urbana: University of Illinois Press.

———— 2012. *Simone de Beauvoir and the Politics of Ambiguity*, Oxford: Oxford University Press.

———— 2022. "Alterity and Intersectionality: Reflections on Old Age in the Time of COVID-19." *Hypatia*, 37: 196–209.

Mann, Bonnie and Martina Ferrari, eds. 2017. "*On ne naît pas femme: on le devient …*" *The Life of a Sentence*. Oxford: Oxford University Press.

McWeeny, Jennifer. 2017. "The Second Sex of Consciousness: A New Ontology and Temporality for Beauvoir's 'Becoming a Woman.'" In "*On ne naît pas femme: on le devient …*" *The Life of a Sentence*, edited by Bonnie Mann and Martina Ferrari, 231–274. Oxford: Oxford University Press.

Marks, Elaine. 1973. *Simone de Beauvoir: Encounters with Death*. New Brunswick: Rutgers University Press.

Moi, Toril. 1990. *Feminist Theory and Simone de Beauvoir*. Oxford: Blackwell.

———— 2008. *The Making of an Intellectual Woman*, Second Edition. Oxford: Oxford University Press.

Murphy, Julien S. 2012. "Introduction." In *Simone de Beauvoir: Political Writings*, edited by Margaret A. Simons and Marybeth Timmerman, 261–271. Urbana: University of Illinois Press.

Nya, Nathalie. 2019. *Simone de Beauvoir and the Colonial Experience: Freedom, Violence, and Identity*. Lanham: Lexington Books.

Picq, Francoise. 2015. "Introduction." *Simone de Beauvoir: Feminist Writings*, edited by Margaret A. Simons and Marybeth Timmerman, 231–239. Urbana: University of Illinois Press.

Schwarzer, Alice. 1984. *After "The Second Sex": Conversations with Simone de Beauvoir*. New York: Pantheon Books.

Simons, Margaret. 1983. "The Silencing of Simone de Beauvoir: Guess What's Missing from The Second Sex." *Women's Studies International Forum*. 6(5): 559–564.

———— 1990. "Sexism and the Philosophical Canon: On Reading Beauvoir's The Second Sex." *Journal of the History of Ideas* 51(3): 487–504.

———— 1999. *Beauvoir and "The Second Sex": Feminism, Race, and the Origins of Existentialism*. Lanham: Rowman and Littlefield.

Spelman, Elizabeth V. 1988. "Simone de Beauvoir: Just Who Does She Think 'We' Is?" In *Inessential Woman: Problems of Exclusion in Feminist Thought*, 57–79, Boston: Beacon Press.

Stavro, Elaine. 1999. "The Use and Abuse of Simone de Beauvoir." *European Journal of Women's Studies* 6(3): 263–280.

Stoller, Silvia, ed. 2014. *Simone de Beauvoir's Philosophy of Age, Gender, Ethics, Time*. Boston: De Gruyter.

Tidd, Ursula. 1999. *Simone de Beauvoir Gender and Testimony*. Cambridge: Cambridge University Press.

Wittig, Monique. 1992. *The Straight Mind and Other Essays*. Boston: Beacon Press.

Young, Iris Marion. 1980. "Throwing Like a Girl: A Phenomenology of Feminine Body Comportment, Motility, and Spatiality." *Human Studies*, 3: 137–156.

INDEX

Printed in the United States
by Baker & Taylor Publisher Services